1. Introduction

I think the hardest part of writing this book is actually getting round to doing the work. When I first began to think about doing it I was completely lost for words. My family and friends that know me well will know what an unusual experience that was for me! What triggered my motivation was reading a book called "An Unexpected Journey" by Margaret Reardon, who had also been married to a man who served in the Colonial Service and her life was so much in parallel with mine that I decided I had better try and put my experiences down as well. I would never have managed it without referring to the letters that I wrote to my parents while I was in Swaziland. Mum diligently kept all my letters and they have helped me to remember so much of that time of my life.

2. From London to Swaziland, via Austria

So I will start at the beginning. I met my husband Ian in Austria. I was on a skiing holiday and he was at the University of Innsbruck doing a course in German. He had just resigned from the Colonial Service where he had served in the Gilbert and Ellis Islands for two tours (see his book called Ghost Stories And Other Island Tales). He had decided that he would never meet a woman who he could get to know, take out and marry when he was living on isolated islands in the western Pacific. I at the time was definitely not interested in being hunted! I was in the middle of my Physiotherapy training in London and I was only 19. He was 30!
I had fallen on the ski slopes in Oberau and managed to land in a heap of cattle dung, which was waiting to be spread over the fields. He had seen it happen and helped me get cleaned up enough to rush back to the hotel. I had to wash my hair (which was long) and having no such thing as a hair dryer, sat in the warm Stube at the Kellerwirt hotel and started writing letters home. I sat next to the Kaggleoven, which was a huge green tiled oven and was wonderfully warm. Ian came in and started asking me what I was doing. He told me to stop doing that and talk to him instead. I told him I was busy and he should go away. One thing about Ian, when he set his mind on something, nothing would distract him. He had already decided that I was to be his wife and set about trying to catch me. He was very persistent. I had to give him that! I had a lovely holiday with him but made him take my friend Beryl with us wherever we went. He taught us how to ski, which I was never any good at but I did try. In those days you stood with your hand above your head and that was how long your skis had to be. They were very long as I am very tall! They did not help my skiing skills at all and many years later when I used the shorter ones I actually became reasonable at skiing. He made us give up ski school and he took us on cross-

country trips. Neither of us was nearly good enough for that but we went anyway and we did have some fantastic experiences. He took us up the mountain called the Schatzberg. In those days there were no lifts so we walked up, taking 4 hours to get to the top walking on skins tied to our skis. We then skied down in something like 10 minutes! Great fun but hair-raising! He also took us to Tierbach, a very small village inaccessible by anything except on foot. We carried our toboggans with us and had a very fast trip down into the Inn valley from where we caught a train to Worgl and then the bus back to Oberau. It was such fun going really fast down a small track. Now one can get to Thierbach very easily and there are wonderful lifts that connect to the Schatzberg.

I had thought this was just going to be one of those holiday romances and that I would never see him again and went back to my digs with my friend Beryl who was from Uganda. The day after we arrived back in London Ian turned up on the doorstep. He insisted that we get married there and then. I refused and told him I simply had to get my training behind me, I was still only 19 and thought that was far too young for marriage. Eventually he went away and found a job in Oswestry where he taught in a boy's school while I was finishing my training. We were married a week after my final exams and I was now 21.

Ian had decided that he really liked working in the Colonial Service and even though he knew the days of Colonial rule were limited he reapplied to get back into the service. He was offered two places, one in Belize and one in Swaziland. We decided that Swaziland sounded a much better option because my parents and family were all in Johannesburg, which was not that far away. So we bought a small car (Sunbeam Rapier with two doors) to take with us and with all our wonderful wedding presents in our container we set off by sea in the Cape Town Castle for Cape Town. That was really our honeymoon as the day after our wedding Ian had to be back at school in Oswestry. It was a lovely trip. There were other members of the Colonial service on board so I began to get a sense of the hierarchy and the protocol that I was going to have to cope with. I had not thought much about my position next to my husband. That journey taught me a lot. There were much more senior people with us who soon put me in my place. Ian and I had a good laugh at one passenger who was traveling with two pretty young women. He told everyone they were his nieces but we could see that this was most certainly not the case!

When the boat docked in Cape Town and we cleared all our possessions including the car we discovered that someone had stolen the windscreen wipers off the car. We knew they had to be replaced as you could get a hefty fine for not having them and the forecast was for rain in the next few days. We were very short of money after the sea voyage, not expecting to have so many extra expenses on board. Ian negotiated a good deal at the garage and we set off with the new wipers fitted. By that stage we had no money at all. Nevertheless we had to get to Swaziland. So we set off anyway and stopped at a hotel somewhere along the N1. We booked ourselves in and then sat on the bed wondering what we should do as we had no money to pay. We both thought it was best to come clean so we asked if we could see the owner and told him about our predicament expecting to be thrown out. He could not have been kinder. He said we could pay him when we could and he even gave us R5.00 for petrol to get as far as Johannesburg where we would be able to ask my parents for help. What a relief and this act of kindness was a fantastic introduction to the kindness and hospitality of South Africans. Needless to say we posted him a check almost the minute we arrived at my parents' house! In those days R5.00 worth of petrol went a long way - I used to pull in and ask for R2.00 super grade, which would fill the tank.

We stayed a few days in Johannesburg where we rested and

saw lots of family and old friends. Those who had not been at our wedding came for a party and we were showered with wonderful gifts from them. My father had not been able to go to England for our wedding so this was his first time to meet Ian. They got on well having had a very similar education at Cambridge University. They always had lots to talk about.

When we set off for Swaziland we knew it would take about 5 hours but what we did not know was how terrible some of the roads were. They were mostly dirt roads heavily corrugated and incredibly dusty. If you had the misfortune to get behind one of the huge South African Railway buses you were covered in a large cloud of dust and could not see anything at all. How we came to hate those buses! We discovered that if you drove at a certain speed you seemed to skim over the corrugations but if you had to slow down for any reason you went into each one and then it became bone shattering.

We had been booked into the hotel in Mbabane and once we had recovered from the journey Ian had to go and make himself known at the Secretariat. He was told that we would be stationed in Stegi, which is a small village near the Mozambique border on the Lebombo hills. It was all new to both of us and we had no idea how far away that was. Actually Swaziland is quite a small country and it is not a very long journey to get anywhere.

That night at our dinner, Ian had ordered York ham, which was on the menu. When he saw the plate of what was clearly not York or any other kind of ham, he told the waiter to take it back as he had ordered York ham. The waiter came back, banged Ian's plate back down and said "chef says York ham". Ian said "no this is not York ham, this is elephant", to which the waiter replied "oh no sir elephant much nicer!" Ian dined out on that story for years! After dinner we were told if we wanted coffee we had to go to another room. We diligently moved to the other room and ordered coffee. When it came we had to pay for it, which Ian did and the waiter took the money and bit it! Well by that time Ian and I were finding it very difficult not to laugh out loud. We had to scuttle off to our room where we wondered what might happen next in this hotel.

"Chef says York ham."

"Elephant is much nicer"

3.   Stegi (now Siteki)

Ian met his new colleagues and we set off for Stegi where he was to be ADC to Owen Strong. Owen was actually just about to leave the service so Ian was able to buy his "ice cream suit" hat and sword, which he would have to wear for ceremonial purposes. The sword was handed over in a tatty old bag and it still lives in the same bag. We were invited to the British High Commissioner's house for lunch. Lady Marwick soon lost interest in me as I had no interest in play-acting. That was her passion. Her husband Sir Brian was a dear man but would soon be retiring.

Stegi was just the most wonderful place to start our time in Swaziland. We had Peter and Bess Forbes as neighbours who were always generous, friendly and hospitable. They had 4 children who rushed over to meet the new neighbours and were bitterly disappointed to find that we had no children. What a blow. They had thought there would be new kids to play with.

Our cottage was a pretty little thatch roofed house with a curved enclosed verandah. It was fully furnished with basic Government Issue, but until our boxes arrived we could not sleep there as we had no bedding or other household goods. I thought it was wonderful and I was so pleased that my very first home would be such a dear little place I was disappointed not to be able to move straight in, but obviously we had to wait for our boxes. So we stayed at the Stegi Hotel and were looked after by Mrs Wiggy (Whigham) who ran the pub. Most of the guests were people going down to Mozambique on business so I did not get to know any people while there. Our house had a lovely view over the lowveld with Erythriner trees flowering profusely.

We had sent out boxes by passenger train, which apparently

we should not have done. It is much cheaper by goods train. Ian had endless arguments with the office about the payment of the expensive one we used. In the end they agreed that we had saved the Government quite a lot of money by receiving our things so quickly which saved us from spending weeks in the hotel!

Once our boxes arrived I started to make a home for us. Ian had not unpacked his boxes after leaving the Gilbert and Ellis Islands so that was my task. My goodness there were some extraordinary things in those boxes. There were things that only bachelors would keep. It was difficult for me to extract any of them from him and I learnt to put up with all this stuff. Grass skirts, woven mats, fans. All of this was interesting but pretty useless to me in the house. Luckily I had brought my sewing machine with me and could make some curtains for the house. I had to convert my sewing machine to being hand-operated, as we had no electricity. One of the gifts we had been given was an electric frying pan, which I exchanged for a battery operated radio and record player.

Our house was on a small hill with the road just below us. The Forbes house was just below us. One morning I woke up to find my garden and the Forbes garden swarming with prisoners. No one had thought to tell me that they did the municipal work like refuse removal and tidying up the street. I got quite a fright, as I was convinced there had been a break out. I learnt later that all the prisoners in Swaziland were expected to work in some way.

We had quite a big garden and I soon bought some seeds and started planting our own vegetables. Our bath water outlet went onto the vegetable garden so I knew we would never be short of water for the vegetables! The little vegetable shop in the village was inadequate and we got very tired of cabbage and tomatoes, which was about all they had. The garden was very fertile and it was soon looking like we could eat our own lettuces and mealies. Until that happened Bess and I would go to her plot where they grew everything they needed. I was allowed to help myself to whatever was ready. The Forbes family were the most generous people and incredibly kind and I really don't know how I would have survived without their help.

There was a small general dealer store in the village. I was used to making out my shopping list, going to the shops and buying what was on my list. This was not going to happen in this shop! The first time I tried to do it my way I wanted to buy chops, potatoes and peas. Not one of those things were available that day or the next. I had to change my whole way of shopping very quickly. I soon discovered the days when chicken might be in, the days when the cheeses arrived, the days the milk and frozen vegetables were delivered. We never had any lamb and I really missed that. The notice outside the shop read "Elizabeth Arden, Stegi, also in London and Paris." I always wished I had a camera and had taken a photo of that.

Shopping was actually quite a challenge. There were no bath or basin plugs in the house. None in the shop either so I had to ask my parents to buy me some and post them down. The bath taps were set incorrectly and would squirt water all over the floor instead of into the bath so I had to ask Mum to buy me some of those rubber extensions for the bath taps. I don't know what I would have done without their help too.

There was no chemist nearby, the nearest being in Manzini. I had to go one day, as we needed something, which I could not get locally. It was only about an hour away but over a very rough road. It was hot in Manzini and I was glad to get back home again where we always seemed to have a bit of a breeze being on the Lebombo range. I heard later that it had been 109 degrees that day. Stegi had been only 95! I had thought it was a bit hot but never realized it was that bad. I dreaded having to live there with that heat.

My flower growing was not as successful as the vegetables, probably because the gardener I had hired was really only interested in food production. I had bought some lovely looking flower seeds from a catalogue, planted them along one wall and up came a whole patch of Zinnias. I would never have bought Zinnias so I knew the person who had lived in the house before me had planted them and I was getting their seeds coming up. Well they were nice and bright! When the rains eventually arrived all kinds of lovely flowers appeared, my favourite being Barberton Daisies. It was terribly dry and the gardens really suffered from lack of rain. Once it rained I found out all about the Stegi mud, which was the stickiest mud I have ever come across. It would cling to your shoes and it was so difficult to get it off.

The car that we had bought was blue and cream two-toned Sunbeam Rapier and very smart. Ian had been assured that there would be servicing available in and around Swaziland for the car. That was not true at all. Not one garage had even heard of such a make of car! So Ian had to teach himself how to do the servicing of this car. He would spend hours tinkering away, greasing the nipples and whatever else had to happen like draining the oil out when it needed changing. The PWD built a horrible corrugated iron garage for the car. I hated the look of it and planted a Golden Shower to grow over it and hide it. They also had dug out a parking space for us. So he was happy there in the shade. His clothes would get filthy and I ended up buying him a brown overall, which I insisted he wore instead of spoiling his better clothes. We were at that stage washing everything by hand having no machine. Betty had come to work for us and she did the washing by hand.

Ian was not highly paid but we really needed a fridge as all the food was going off without one. My milk would turn sour every day and I had to make cottage cheese with it but we did need to make a plan. We bought a small paraffin fridge using one whole month's salary and then I wondered how I would be doing the shopping. It was easy actually as both the vegetable shop and the store worked on a tick (credit) system and I was able to put everything on tick until the end of the month. I did not like doing that as I had never lived on that sort of system but it did work. My father would have been horrified as we were taught to only buy what you could afford so that you never owed anyone money.

We had to buy a paraffin fridge because we had no electricity. Our lights were Tilly lamps, which Ian had used in the Gilbert and Ellis Islands. They gave a very good light while making a gentle hissing noise. Unfortunately they would smoke every night and so each morning we had to clean the chimneys and trim the wick. However hard I tried to trim the wick they still smoked badly. The paraffin fridge also had a chimney which required cleaning every week. The fuel tank needed to be filled once a week and it was my job to get it out and fill it. Not a job I enjoyed! We had a gas cooker. I had never cooked on gas before so that was quite a learning curve for me with naturally plenty of burnt food. We had an old donkey boiler outside the back door, which heated the bath water and the kitchen water. The gardener's duty was to light a fire under it every morning and again in the evening if it had gone out. The dustbin and gas cylinders were also outside the back door and I found that snakes used to like being either under the bin or draped somewhere near the boiler. I would keep my distance and never killed them. There were lots of black mambas at certain times of the year and we seemed to be right in their path between their wintering grounds and where they hung out in summer. There were frightening stories about them in the village. On the wall of the club was a picture of a black mamba with a round ball shaped lump in its body. It must have swallowed a golf ball!

Ian used to walk to the office through the golf course. It was a lovely walk and he enjoyed it. He told me he always saw something interesting along the way. I was hoping it would not be a mamba. The first time he saw a Hadeda Ibis he was alarmed by the noise they made. They really just said very loudly "ha ha deda!" He told someone at the office about them and they told him the name of the bird. We had been given a bird book and I think that Ibis sighting triggered our interest in birds. We heard Egyptian geese each morning and again in the evenings.

I said the boiler heated our water system, but that was of course only on the days when we had water. We would always be told which days of the week the water would be turned on. I used to fill buckets up to use on the days when there was no water. Sometimes it was very chlorinated and Ian would say that was because the man in charge had forgotten the dose yesterday so doubled it up the next day. We had been advised not to drink the tap water. There was no such thing as bottled water at that time so we boiled our water every day, cooled it off and used that. This became a habit, which we kept up all the time we were in Swaziland. Sometimes the water was a terrible dark colour. Especially when we were waiting for rain and the dam was very low.

Ian used to go out into the bush to inspect the dams and he came home one day saying that they were all terribly low and we had to have rain soon or the farmers would be in deep trouble. Luckily it did start to rain soon after that. He took me on his court days to Lomahasha, which was on the Mozambique border. I was left with the wife of the local stock inspector. She was delighted to have a visitor and talked all day long! I think she had a very lonely life. She had a new batch of sweet kittens and we were promised one of them when it was big enough to leave the mother. They were all covered in fleas and once we got the kitten it was my difficult job to try and deflea her. We called her Flit as this is the product we used to spray for mosquitoes and fleas!

There was an active and very social club in the village. I think some of the old timers were pretty used to having lots of alcohol. I was not, and they soon realized I was nowhere near their league. They soon stopped even trying to make me drink. They thought I was very odd only drinking tonic water. Ian of course could hold his own against any of them and I think that impressed them. I would have rather not have them impressed by something like that. There were a pair of women who were friends of Bess Forbes called Mitzy and Thurl. I don't think I have ever before or since seen women with that capacity for booze without any sign of inebriation at all.

I decided that I had better go and introduce myself to some of my neighbours. I walked along one day to see the Aldwinkles. He was a pilot and he flew me to Johannesburg one day much later on in my stay. When I knocked on the door she thought I was a school child coming to beg money off them and was just about to see me off when I told her who I was. She was astounded. She said "But I thought you were a school girl." I was still only 21 and I suppose to her I did look very young! She gave me some of the most marvellous fruitcake and gave me the recipe.

The policeman in the village was Altham Tainton and he and his wife June were both very welcoming. They were the only other young couple in the village. June came from Scotland and became a great friend. She had a little boy called Gordon. I really enjoyed having the youngster around. I found that time was heavy on my hands in Stegi because I was not working so Ian and I decided to start our family straight away. I had a little morning sickness and was beginning to think that I might be pregnant. My mother had sent me a telegram to ask if it was alright for them to come and see us. She asked because my brothers had been in contact with German measles and might go down with it. I was not really sure if I was pregnant so I said yes it was fine to come. They came and both boys went down with the German measles. I went to see the doctor at the local clinic in Stegi. He was Polish and his name was Whiskey Willie. It wasn't of course but that was what we all called him having one of those complicated unpronounceable Polish ones! He could not speak English. Neither could the Italian nun nor the Swazi sister. So I had to explain in my very best sign language that I thought maybe I was pregnant and all the business about my brothers. It was not easy but eventually dawn broke and Whiskey Willie understood what I was trying to tell him. He gave me a Gamma Globulin injection (most painful!) to stop me from catching it. He had first established that I was actually 6 weeks pregnant! Best not to catch the measles as it can affect the baby. The reason the injection was so painful was because the liquid is very thick and had to go through a needle that you might use on a horse by the look of it!

My brothers loved their trip. They were 13 and 15 and they had never met Ian. He greatly impressed them when he shot a boomslang in the tree above our heads. We had gone down to the lowveld where there was a lot of game and which has subsequently been made into a game reserve called Hlane. Ian had seen two poachers with a carcass of an impala on their shoulders running away. He made the mistake of throwing a stone at them to try and make them stop for questioning. They are far better shots than he ever would be and he got quite a crack on his arm from a well-aimed stone, when they threw a stone back at him. I don't think he ever challenged a poacher quite like that again.

We were so lucky that my parents lived in Johannesburg, which was close enough for us to go and stay with them for a long weekend. The roads were terrible and if it had been raining we used to have a very slippery trip back. There was often a lot of thick mist when we drove through the Usutu forest and that was quite scary especially at night. I used to do my shopping on these trips and that helped a lot.

There was not much in the way of entertainment in Stegi. Every now and then there would be a film show held at the club. It was projected onto a wall and of course there had to be a few breaks while they changed the film. We all made a beeline to the pub for drinks. Some people would knock back 4 or 5 crème de menthes during the short interval. All I ever needed was something cold as it was very hot in that room. I saw some wonderful old films there and enjoyed the evenings very much. One evening at the club Peter Forbes came in and told Tommy Boothe that he was in breach of club regulations. Tommy was flustered and said, "Why on earth would that be?" Peter hauled out a long green snake from Tommy Boothe's golf bag and put it on the bar counter saying he was keeping pets in the club. He was apt to do this kind of thing and was often teasing people with snakes. Well he certainly got the desired reaction. All the women jumped onto the bar counter, Tommy fled and Peter just laughed. The snake was dead and was a harmless one anyway. I don't think any of us really forgave Peter that joke!

While we were living in Stegi, one day when Bess and Peter were going to Manzini they hit a wildebeest and the car was damaged so while they were sitting on the side of the road waiting for help, Bess sat on the carcass and began to feed her baby. A tourist vehicle came by with Americans in it. One of them wanted to know all about "this here moose" and asked questions about why it was dead. Peter told him he had shot it and that they were going to feed the moose to the baby. The Americans believed him and gave him a very old fashioned look.

Feeding "this here moose" to the baby

Another of Peter's pranks was when a lot of the men had been having a very drunken party. One of the policemen had a gone staggering off to bed a bit the worse for wear. Peter had put the head of a dead Zebra into his bed and when he tried to get into bed he sort of shoved it up and told to it move over. He slept all night with it next to him and when he woke up he thought he was having nightmares or DTs or something terrible. He swore he would never get so drunk again!

There was a farmer in the district called Fireball Elliot. I never discovered his real name, and I never knew why he was called Fireball. One night during one of his heavy drinking parties the men were boasting about their shooting prowess. Fireball woke his gardener up and made him bring his very expensive and rare Rhode Island Red hens. He made the man throw them up into the air and he shot each one. The next day he wanted to kill that poor gardener!

Ian decided that I had to learn how to play bridge to keep us busy in the evenings. I had never played before and found it a most complicated game. I was never any good at it but tried my best and went along as his partner. We would travel miles over dreadful roads for him to get a game. One place we used to go to was in the lowveld at Big Bend where there was a big community of sugar farmers. They were good fun to play with because they did not take it all that seriously. However I was always doing the wrong thing, revoking or some other such dreadful sin and Ian would tick me off. When we left Swaziland I refused to ever play again as I had hated playing so much. Ian was surprised so I was glad that I had disguised it so well. I remember playing with a couple that was very good. She was French and he was English. I learned a lot of very French nasty swearwords from her. I had never heard anyone called those words before. I felt really sorry for her husband who endured all this abuse. She thought I could not understand French but I could and I knew very well that what she was saying was pretty rude. I think bridge brings out the worst in some people! Ian's father played a lot and one day someone was bidding up and up until she got to seven no trumps when she declared "And you can't go higher than that!"

We kept on hearing about the wonderful prawns to be had in Lourenco Marques (now Maputo). Ian worked out that if we left early in the morning we could get there, eat some prawns and be back in time for the border closing at 6.00 pm. We went one day and it was tremendous fun. We decided that we would go again but I think it took us a while to get back there as it was quite an expensive day for us. They were building a railway line between L.M. and Swaziland for the iron ore. There was a couple we got to know in the village. He was working on the line and promised Ian he would take him to see it one day. It was terribly hot where they were working and one of the big wigs came to see the work in progress .The temperature was 119 degrees and he passed out from the heat and when he came back to Stegi he ordered a crate of cold beers to be sent to the chaps on the line. He felt so sorry for them in that heat. They were working in a river gorge and it could get extremely uncomfortable there. There will be more about the railway line later.

One of the neighbours along the road was Annie Cook. She was American and a widow. She was lovely and always good fun and she played a lot of bridge. Her house was big and had a wonderful view down across the lowveld. She used to like sitting on her verandah and watching the bush below her house. I never found out how she came to be living in Stegi.

Another of the old Stegi residents was Joyce Boothe. She was married to Tommy Boothe. I think they were the mainstay of the club bar. They were kind and hospitable. I found everyone in Stegi very welcoming to us. They were happy to have new people to talk to and made an effort to see that we enjoyed ourselves there. Joyce took me to visit her daughter who was married to a sugar farmer in the lowveld. There were lots of canals all full of water and as we drove by we saw hordes of locals swimming and washing in the canals. It looked as if they really enjoyed having so much water! Before the canals were built they would have had only the river and that would have been full of crocodiles.

Ian really never spoke much about his work but I know he was getting on well with his colleagues in the office. Owen Strong left soon after we arrived and Ian was then Acting District Commissioner. That commanded a certain respect from his staff. He had to learn to speak Swazi as part of his promotion incentive. So he really tried hard. He was never a good linguist but he did his best to communicate with the Swazis that came to see him in the office. He did pass the exams eventually and was duly promoted but that was much later. I think the best part of his job was going out into the rural areas and getting to know the local folk there. They had a very good agricultural department and he used to go out with them where they talked to the chiefs about overgrazing and good tick management as well as good farming practices. One of his jobs was to inspect the prison and listen to any complaints that the prisoners might have. One day he and Whisky Willie were doing the inspection together when one prisoner said he had a complaint about the food, most especially about the beans they were given. He had a handful of beans, which he showed them and said they were far too hard. Whisky Willie picked one up and ate it saying there was nothing wrong with the beans. The prisoner said "yes, but it has been through me once already!" They had to count the number of Prisoners present and some days the numbers were too many and some too few. Ian asked why that happened and was told that the prisoners would go to another prison if they needed to be near home or they just felt like a change! It was all pretty porous.

4.   To the bright lights of Mbabane

I had settled into a happy routine in Stegi. I had made good friends. I could manage the shopping. Flit had settled well into being our cat. She was sweet and used to like to sleep in the wash basket. All this was not to last though. Ian came back from work one day to tell me that he had been transferred to Mbabane to the Secretariat. I was very sad to leave Stegi. My garden was just starting to be productive. I would miss June who, soon after we left was transferred to a very isolated Lowveld police station where things were very hard for her. At least I was going to civilisation! We only lived in Stegi for four months and I thought it was such a shame to leave it. We had made lovely friends there who we did keep in touch with and who would visit us later in our other postings.

Ian took me to Lourenco Marques at the weekend for my birthday treat. It was our last weekend in Stegi. We went to have prawns to eat and then in the evening we went to the famous nightclubs enjoying the bright lights. Ian said he was not impressed by the nightclub but I loved it. I had never been to one before!

When it was time to start packing I was allocated some prisoners who loaded a small PWD lorry up with our possessions and we set off for Mbabane. Ian had not been feeling well so I had to do all the packing myself. When we got there we heard that the house we were supposed to be going into had been allocated to someone else and we would have to stay in a flat until a house became available. That was a huge disappointment to me but I made the best of it and unpacked our things and made the flat comfortable. It was really rather a terrible little flat but what could we do? Ian was now really feeling ill and had to go to see a doctor who found that he had mumps. He was to stay in bed for at least 3 days. So he did not start his new job when he should have. He was given a rather cool welcome as a result. I am not sure about this but I don't think he liked working in the Secretariat as much as in the district.

It took a while for a house to become vacant for us but when it was ready we had the prisoners back again to help us to move into the new house. There was only one spare room as the person who lived in it was on leave and had left all his things in one bedroom. We had to wait for him to come back from leave to get the bedroom back. This is how it worked in Swaziland and we left our gear in bedrooms later on when we went on leave. It was a surprise to me all the same! We moved in on 15th December and had to really hurry to get everything ship shape as Ian's Uncle Teddy was to arrive on 17th. We were to spend Christmas with my parents and take Uncle Teddy with us. I had managed to make the Christmas cake quickly before we left Stegi. We took Uncle Teddy to the Bushman's Rock hotel which was a lovely spot on a hill near White River. From there we could go to the Kruger Park on a daily basis. We had luck there and saw masses of wild life.

Ian's new job was very different now. They were preparing the Budget in England and he seemed to be spending hours on that as he kept getting urgent telegrams about needing estimates for this or that, having waited three months before answering his last correspondence. I had the feeling he did not like his job much. He took Uncle Teddy off to see the iNcwala which is a Swazi ceremony during which there is a lot of dancing and sweating. I had a quiet afternoon at home by choice. We always had to go to the Residency to meet hundreds of disinterested people at cocktail parties for some important person. I did not enjoy them at all. They usually only served vodka or Portuguese wine neither of which I liked. Ian was very happy to use my "delicate" health as an excuse not to stay late!

We both noticed the difference in the air in Mbabane. It was fresh and cool. The house was lovely and had a well-established garden but it was badly in need of cutting back straggly growth. I found that compost making was really easy there as the climate was just right so I had a wonderful compost pit going soon. The house looked out over a valley and there was a good tar road not far away, which led to town. I settled in quickly and started setting about making this house into a comfortable home. There were only the two bedrooms so I made one into a nursery for this new baby on the way. My mother gave me the old bassinet that all five of us had used as babies. I covered it with white cotton and made a mosquito net to go over it.

While I was unpacking Ian came in to fetch a picnic I had made for him to take on his trip to do an inspection with a soil specialist. Just after they had left they came back and asked me if I would like to go too. So I dropped what I had been doing and went with them, thoroughly enjoyed the outing. The road was very rough and only accessible with a 4 wheel drive vehicle. We saw a troop of baboons and we were told there were a lot of crocodiles and hippos in the Usutu river at Abercorn drift, which was where we had our picnic. It was very wild country and I would say was full of other wild life. We saw lots of beautiful wild flowers and I knew that I would need a book to help me identify them. There used to be a pont there at one time. It was only 900 feet elevation and was very hot and sticky. There was a mango tree near the river and we each had a sweet mango with our lunch! I picked up some lovely red jasper from the edge of the river there.

We were given a puppy one day. It was very small, black and of unknown origin but could become quite a big dog by the look of its feet. We called him Scratch (because he was always scratching!) and he was well entrenched in the house before the baby was born. A delightful little dog but was terrified of thunder and would climb into the cupboards under the sink if he heard any thunder about.

Our next-door neighbours welcomed us and Creina and I became great friends. Her husband, Greville Beatie, was an insurance salesman at that stage. We had to ask him to stop trying to sell us insurance if we were to stay friends. He was very good about that and never bore a grudge against us. We used to play bridge with them and one night found out that Ted Reilly was a relation of Creina's. It was through them that we got to know Ted and Liz and became interested in Mlilwane Game reserve. They moved later on into a beautiful house above Mbabane where they could have horses and chickens. He had a butchery at one time and gave me a marvellous sharp butchers knife. They had three children Craig, Debbie and Lee.

My pregnancy was advancing. There had been no access to any form of antenatal advice, assistance or medical care at all in Stegi. So now that I was in a big town I first of all bought Dr Spock. This is the book about child raising that I am afraid we all brought our babies up on. He had some very strange ideas about caring for babies and they are not what people think are correct now! I went to see a doctor at the Government hospital. That was such a bad experience that I never bothered to go back until the baby was due. I decided as I was a qualified Physiotherapist, I ought to know enough to see that I stayed healthy. I bought the right kind of vitamins and iron and did it my way. I joined an antenatal class where I met and made friends with other women who would eventually become life friends. I recently met up with Marjorie James who had been in my class and we picked our friendship back up again.

The Swaziland Radio station was just being inaugurated while we were there and I was asked if I would like to present a program of my favourite music one day. I loved doing it and got out my old records and chose a selection of songs that I thought would be popular. I had some good Negro Spiritual music and some nice sea shanties as well as some West End

Shows. They seemed to like what I compiled and said that they had enjoyed them all.

One day when I was in town trying to shop in the butchery and feeling very nauseous I had to go outside to be quietly sick in the gutter. A woman came up to me very sympathetic and said "oh you poor dear you must be pregnant." It was an old school friend of mine Angela Lemon. She was now Angela Kernot and her husband Peter was a muleteer and worked in the Usutu forest with the mules. It was so lovely to make contact with her again and we were to see lots of them during our time in Swaziland. Isn't it funny how you can pick up an old friendship so easily just as if you have never been apart? Well I can anyway.

Ian wanted to go to Kosi Bay and stay there for the Easter weekend. We got as far as Ndumu Game Reserve and found they did not sell petrol and that the road to Kosi Bay was impassable except for 4 wheel drive vehicles. So we camped outside the park (which we found out later was illegal!) I had a sleepless night hearing every noise outside, hippos, impalas rutting, and a thousand other unidentifiable noises. Also despite having piles of soft things for me to sleep on, the ground felt as hard as nails. However we did get a drive through the park (for 5 shillings each!) in a land rover. The young man took us right round the lake and we saw hundreds of crocodiles and wonderful bird life. We stayed one more night in our illegal camping ground but I am afraid I refused to sleep in the tent for another night and we had to go to Mkuse where we found a hotel for me. Ian was rather disgusted at me for being so fragile about it all, but I was 6 months pregnant at the time! Ndumu was wonderful though and although we only drove through it we decided it would be worth going back again but making a proper booking this time. The Natal Parks Board ran it and the lake was full of hippos and crocodiles. There were huge old fig trees around the edge of the lake and the bush beyond that looked interesting with a variety of trees which we were not familiar with. We saw some good bird life there too so knew we would be back again one day. Mkuse was also very interesting and had a far better road system so we thought we should go back there one day too.

This baby of mine was due in the beginning of June. I was enormous and starting to be very uncomfortable. There had been some unrest in Swaziland and certain demands had been made which had not been met. I think they were demanding a pound a day wage and Ian and all the office staff were all on night-time stand by duty to protect the neighbourhood. He had to patrol our street until they were sure all was quiet. He taught me how to use our shot gun, "just in case". It gave a huge kick to your shoulder when you pulled the trigger and I was sure I would never hit anything anyway. I was not happy to learn but he insisted I knew what to do. So you can picture a hugely pregnant woman firing off an ancient shotgun for protection! All the men on our patrol were told to keep an eye out for me when they drove past the house just in case I needed a lift to the hospital.

The unrest did not settle down so the British troops who were stationed in Kenya were ordered down to Swaziland to protect the Colony. They had been fighting a really horrible battle there and were rather bloodthirsty Gordon Highlanders. Most of them were tough Glaswegians who arrived with their bayonets practically at the ready and loved the idea that they would be in a raging battle very soon. I think the Swazi agitators took one look and stood down quickly. The place where the worst of the agitation had taken place was on a bridge across the river and that road was the one I would need to take if I was to get to the hospital.

Well this baby was reluctant to put in an appearance and I was admitted when I was two weeks overdue for an induction. Nothing happened so I came home and waited another week. The induction worked this time and an exhausted little boy Tom was born eventually. I remember his cry sounding just like a starling. It was a long and difficult birth and I overheard the doctor discussing the possibility of doing a Caesar but was told the theatre was not ready. She gave up on me and called in another doctor, Ian Tait who bulldozed me into getting on with the job of delivering this child. He was wonderful and I liked him tremendously. Subsequently he became our doctor. I can't say anything good about that hospital. It was so terrible that I said if I had another baby it would never be born there. The injection site became seriously infected so I went home with dressings and a very sore bottom.

Before Tom was born I was in town waddling along looking huge. Some of the soldiers passed me and whistled at me. I was so taken aback! I thought I looked so terrible but they obviously thought I looked alright! Those soldiers had a great time in Mbabane. There was a man who owned the hotel who had a problem with his Eustachian tubes and if he held his nose and took a mouth full of liquid (usually beer!) he could blow it out if his ear. That was such fun and he made a fortune out of that trick by betting the soldiers that he could do it! They had never seen anything like that before. They had a lot of fun in Mbabane and I have a feeling there were a few blue eyed little babies around after they left.

Tommy was a very easy baby and he used to sleep outside in his pram under the tree in the garden. That was where we used to have tea with other mothers and their babies. I have a lovely photo of Marjorie and June with Alison and Richard sitting on my lawn with Tommy. Gordon was toddling around in the background. It was an easy life. As soon as I was well enough I started to work because I really wanted to have some money saved so that if I had another baby I could go into the new private nursing home called St Michaels. So I started treating patients at the house. My most regular one was a man called Ian Aires who had worked in Tanganyika.

He was interesting and talked fondly about his time there. He didn't seem to mind Tom in his playpen nearby either. We called anyone who had worked elsewhere in Africa a "When we" because of them telling us about their time there! I suppose its hard not to do that! Ian Aires was definitely a "When we."

Tommy needed to be taken to see a doctor in South Africa urgently. I was booked to fly with him on the diplomatic flight, which sounded very grand. I expected a big plane and when we got the airport was shocked to see a small dinky airplane waiting for me. It was Mr. Aldwinkle from Stegi who was the pilot and he flew us to the Wonderboom airfield outside Pretoria. He flew by looking at the roads below us and navigating the way by turning when the road turns. We sort of hopped over the Usutu forest and I could see the wood workers below very clearly. It was quite an experience! My mother met us at the Wonderboom airfield (which was really a military airfield) and she took me back later to catch the plane home. Going home I sat next to Mr.Todd an important politician in Swaziland. He tried to be very intimidating, making remarks about having a baby on board his flight, but I was having none of that and ignored him.

We decided to go to Xai Xai in Mozambique six weeks after Tommy was born. He was such an easy baby I knew he would be no problem and I was right. He slept all the way there and back. Xai Xai is north of Lourenco Marques and to get there you have to cross a wide river (the Limpopo), which does not have a bridge. They had a pontoon to get the cars across and the lads pulling the ropes chanted in rhythm a lovely song about the people from Swaziland traveling with a tiny baby! They beat the deck with their feet at the same time. It was great fun. The hotel did not amount to much. It was a typical concrete structure with no character that the Portuguese always seemed to build along that coast. But the food was excellent and we ate a lot of seafood. Ian sat out on the reef and ate as many oysters as he could find! There were a lot of families with children staying at the hotel, mostly Rhodesians and South Africans so that was a nice change for us.

My aunt and uncle Patricia and Dennis Anderson came to see us for a few days. They were based in Northern Rhodesia where he was a policeman. They brought their small daughter Mary with them so Tommy and Mary got to meet each other when they were very little. There is a bit of a generation gap here as Patricia was my mother's youngest sister and she was having her family at the same time as me. Mary was a dear little girl and was fun to have in the house. While they were with us I heard from my sister Ellen who had just moved to Borneo where her husband Jeff worked for Shell. She was telling me about her shopping and it sounded so much better than ours! The oil tankers brought all the food over and she could even get Birds eyes peas! Patricia said it sounded even better than her shops up north.

My garden needed some new plants so I went over to Stegi with Diana Simkin and we raided my old garden for some plants. We then drove back to Manzini and met up with Ian and Peter who had been playing squash there. We had a prawn meal at the Portuguese restaurant in Manzini and had a great evening with them. What was good about living in Mbabane from my point of view was the fact that I could make friends with people who were not in Government service. Marjorie and Chris James were living and working in Swaziland. He was a geologist and was working in the mining industry. Marjorie was in my antenatal classes and her baby Alison was born a few weeks before my baby and June Tainton also had a baby at about this time. June had a hard time living where Al had been posted, as there was no water at all in her house. An old donkey cart delivered her water supply and she had to boil it all. Even the baby's bath water had to be boiled first. At least we had a steady water supply in Mbabane.

We had been in Mbabane for a few months and it was Christmas time soon. Ian had asked if we could go and visit his friend Ted Nettleton who was the Distinct Commissioner in Mokhotlong in Lesotho. Ted was happy for us to come. We realised that it would be quite a trip, as we had to go up the Sani pass to get there. We had heard about this amazing pass and were keen to see it. That was the only way to get to that part of Lesotho. It meant taking a Landover from the Sani Pass hotel to Mokhotlong. Doesn't that sound so easy! The Landrover did not look to me to be in very good condition. I had to hold the door closed next to me every time we went round a corner or it would swing open. I had Tommy, then about 6 months on my lap and Ian sat next to the driver and we set off. None of us had seat belts! They were unheard of then. The back of the Landrover was full of coal and other essential supplies for the folk at the top. The journey was wonderful from one point of view. The views were stunningly beautiful, but the road was hazardous and quite terrifying. The hairpin bends were very sharp and some of them had to be negotiated by doing a three-point turn to get round the bend. The edges of the road were close and the drop was enormous. So, holding onto the baby and the door we made our way to the border control at the top of the pass. When we got there a very smart policeman greeted us and asked us where we had come from and furthermore where were we going to. Since there is only one road and it came from the bottom and went to the top I could not see why he asked us that! It seemed pretty obvious to me. We had a pit stop at the border post. They offered us a cup of tea, which we had, but as I really don't like condensed milk in my tea I could not drink it. I was still at the stage of feeling rather morning sick with the next baby so I am afraid I had to pour mine out. The driver went away to have some other kind of liquid refreshment and when he came back to the Landrover he was pretty drunk. We still had another 4 hours at least on the road so had to endure an extremely bad road with a very inebriated driver. It was not at all funny and Ian and I were relieved when we arrived after an 8-hour journey at Mokhotlong. Ted and his wife Gail were very welcoming. I don't think they had many visitors there. They put us up in a little Rondavel in the garden, which was very comfortable, and being far away from the house we knew the baby would not disturb them. Ted and Ian went off on horseback to go fishing one day. They came home with some wonderful fresh trout from the streams up there, the altitude being right for trout. The climate at Christmas time was lovely and since they had a pool in the garden we cooked the trout on an open fire next to the pool and that was our Christmas meal. It was delightful. Gail's kitchen was interesting. There was a huge fireplace with enough space inside to hang a couple of hams to smoke in it. These people who administered this part of Lesotho had very little access to any fresh food and had to be pretty well self-sufficient. I really admired the way they had to live. To get anywhere in the district was arduous and difficult for Ted and he relied on his horses. The road to Maseru was only just passable and not all the year round. I thought I had it really easy in Swaziland when I saw what Gail had to cope with! Ian was out in the sun far too long one day when they were out riding and went down with sunstroke. We had to call a doctor who came from the clinic and made the diagnosis. He said he saw it frequently as people don't realise how strong the sun is at that altitude.

I started playing tennis soon after we got home again and enjoyed getting the exercise as well as seeing lots of other people. The Taintons were back in Mbabane and June introduced me to some more of the police wives. Sonia Everett had a baby just before Tom so she was a good person for advice. She and Steve had 4 children eventually but at that time she just had Susan and Sally. June's baby Richard had survived living in his very primitive surroundings and he and Gordon were often at our house visiting. We had also met and liked very much John and Jeanette Sturgis. He was a magistrate and she was a draughtswoman in town. They lived on a farm in the Ezulwini valley just below Mbabane. Jeanette had been married before and was a widow. She had only just married John when we met them. She had three sons who evidently needed a man's influence. That must have been her motivation to marry John! Her first husband had been a wild Irishman called Peter O Kelly. I think some of the boys were rather like their father.

We had some good evenings at their house. Jeanette was a brilliant cook as having a French father she was keen on her food. Ian and John got on really well together. Both had an acerbic streak and they would lead each other on in various discussions. I found that very tedious! I remember my children being most impressed by her boys especially the one who wiped his hands on his hair after eating a mango!

Benson joined us after a while in Mbabane. He was a schoolboy and it was the custom for people to take in a schoolchild who came from a rural area and would not normally have access to school. Benson turned up one day and we hired him. He was such a nice youngster. He went to school every day and afterwards would clean all our shoes and then work in the garden. I had to teach him which plants were which but he never had to be shown twice. We gave him a small wage, which I am sure he sent straight back to his family. I also had acquired a new domestic, as Betty had not come with us from Stegi. Her name was Ida Momane Dlamini and she was a princess. When she put on all her Swazi regalia she looked wonderfully royal. Ida was a very bright, happy person and was far better at housework than I had ever been. I taught her how to cook and she became a very good cook. She was brilliant with the baby and was altogether a most satisfactory staff member. She stayed with us the whole time we were in Swaziland and followed us faithfully to each posting. Benson did too and just swapped schools!

5. Manzini

Ian came in from work one evening with the look on his face, which I now knew. We were to be transferred to Manzini. Once again I had to brace myself for another move. I was very sorry that I would be leaving this bunch of nice new friends. And my garden was once again just starting to be really productive. Making compost in that garden was so easy. The climate was just right and I had plenty of vegetables in just a few weeks. Mbabane was a very nice place to live. It had a good climate and there was a lot to do. There was an amateur dramatic society which managed to produce some very good shows. Jeanette was involved with that and we saw her acting her parts very well. There was even a cinema and we saw the first James Bond Movie there. John Sturgis took us and we laughed all the way through.

The neighbours had a cat that used to come over and spend time at our house. One evening I had spent a while cleaning a fish for supper. I left it on a plate and went to lie down and when I came back it had gone! The cat had eaten the whole fish leaving me just the bones. Our cat Flit loved prawns and we had to watch her like a hawk while we were eating them or the same thing would happen.

When we moved this time we needed a slightly bigger PWD lorry since we had increased our family and our possessions. This time the house we were allocated was a drab little place at the bottom of the long hill from Stegi. There was a traffic circle at the bottom of this hill and the traffic noise was dreadful. There was a nice jacaranda tree in the garden and Ian put up a swing for Tommy on one of the branches. That became a great favourite. I had never really liked the idea of living in Manzini on account of that hot day I spent in town doing the shopping. We were going into summer time and it got progressively warmer. I got used to the heat and soon learned the best way of keeping the house cool, shutting the curtains early in the morning and opening them at night.

I was once again pregnant but I had not disclosed this to anyone yet. I had to go into the chemist shop one day and one of the ladies talking to the pharmacist said her child had German measles. It was the child that was holding her hand in the shop. Well, I ran out of the shop so fast but heard someone say as I ran out "Marion must be pregnant judging by her reaction!" So word was out now and I could now let everyone know.

I had been determined to never go back into the Government hospital but still had not saved up quite enough to go to the Private clinic so I applied for a job at The Raleigh Fitkin Hospital. I worked every day for a few hours. This hospital was run by American Missionaries. They were wonderful people and I went there for all my antenatal appointments although they knew I would not deliver in their hospital. The doctors were kind and efficient. I really enjoyed that work as I could go into the wards and treat the long-term orthopaedic patients. I had to learn a bit more Swazi to be able to communicate with the patients although there was always a sister to help me if I needed it. I used to have a cup of tea with the wives of the doctors before going home. There was always a nice little piece of cake for me too.

Ian was the Assistant District officer and his immediate superior and D.C. was Jack Edwards and he and his wife Joan lived in the District Commissioner's house along the road from us. The Chief Justice lived next door to them. I used to walk to town if I needed anything and had to pass these smart houses. I wondered if we would ever live in such a nice house! The shops in Manzini were good and certainly much better than what I had been used to in Stegi. There was quite a big supermarket. One day when I was pretty far gone in my pregnancy I tripped up and fell down just outside the shop. The local people in the street could not have been kinder and helped me up and took me home again.

When the time came for the new baby to be born I refused to go into the hospital until I was at least 3 weeks overdue. I was lucky with the doctor Ian Tait who knew me well and did not insist that I try after a week or even two weeks. He was ready for me in St Michaels and gave me the injection I seemed to always need to get labour going. Jane was born later that evening and what a beautiful little baby she was too. The midwife who attended me was an old school friend Margaret Summers. I was so pleased to see a familiar face then. We had dropped Tommy off at the Sturgis house. Jeanette had offered to take care of him while I was in hospital. Ian was not around as he had been offered a trip on the new railway to Mozambique which had just been built and was at last through the gorge. He had been promised this trip for a long time and did not want to lose the opportunity. He was never any good at hospitals or illness anyway so I did not mind. While I was in the hospital it must have been when Jane was about three days old my Doctor came in to see me very late one evening. He was very upset, as he had just been dealing with the murder of the Minister of Finance Bob Martin. Bob had answered the door when the doorbell rang and a man demanded money, as he was the minister of finance and must surely have lots available. When Bob told the man he had none he shot him. Such a sad loss for his family and such a terrible loss for the Secretariat too.

When Jane was settled in the routine of feeding we left the hospital and picked Tommy up at Jeanette and went home to Manzini. Tommy was still very little and had no difficulty welcoming his new sister. Jane was another very easy baby and was a real delight. She was standing very early and learned to walk at about 9 months. I had a pram now and would put both babies into the pram for any shopping expeditions. I had to leave the house really early to be back before it got too hot to be outside. We now had electricity and

I decided that we ought to try and buy a washing machine as we had all these nappies to wash every day. I managed to get a second hand one. It was a small Hoover with only one tub and a mangle that you used to squeeze out the water. It was wonderfully efficient and Ida appreciated not having to do the washing by hand any more. Yes it was Terry towelling nappies then. The disposable ones had not really been introduced yet. The only time I used them was when we were flying home and they gave Jane a terrible rash so I never used them again.

The British Army had a base in Manzini now and was a presence in town. We used to have some of the young officers over for meals and they loved seeing the children. They had a special parade of some importance to the regiment and we were invited. My friend Angela came with me. I was a spectator and I suppose Ian was on the podium. The Swazi regiment who had also been invited came on to the parade ground playing their largely home made musical instruments. The cacophony was to us very normal. The soldiers who were standing at attention couldn't believe their ears and eyes! The Swazis were in traditional gear and that is not very much in the way of clothing. The music is very different and the young soldiers had great difficulty keeping to attention and not breaking ranks. I saw some of them with their shoulders heaving with suppressed laughter. They had evidently not been warned about what they might see that day. The regimental silver was on the tables and I overheard the mess officer telling the lads to put it away quickly. He was not having any of it disappearing. Glasses of gin, brandy and whiskey had been poured and I watched one man pour four tots, all different, into one glass and swig that off! There was food on the tables as well and I watched with horror as the women filled their handbags with all the small canapés. They would clearly need to be advised about the protocol of such functions.

"Quick lads, hide the silver!"

Keeping the mess silver in the regiment

Angela and her husband Peter were now farming near Manzini. They had a smallholding and were growing avocado pears. They lived in a shed, not having the money to build a house. The 7-day war broke out in the Middle East and Peter had the foresight to realise that the U.K would not be able to import avocados from Israel while that was going on. He quickly reaped his whole crop, packed it up and flew the boxes to the U.K. They made enough money to pay for the house to be built! He said it was just good timing on his part! I was so pleased for Angela as she was finding it very hard living in that shed.

Tommy needed a bit of socialising so I went to see a lady I had heard was running a small nursery school from home. He was very little still which she was not all that happy about but when she saw how he loved playing with the other children she allowed him to come for a few hours three times a week. I would drop him off with a change of clothes and nappies and fetch him after I had finished work. He thrived on it and Sheena who ran the school became a good friend. So did Sue Hill who was her teacher. Sue was married to Doug Hill who was a policeman and we got to know them very well too. Sheena's husband was Harry Shirley and he was an architect and very keen on amateur dramatics. They were a great couple with a lovely sense of humour and they also had children the same age as ours. They had come from Nyasaland (now called Malawi).

6. Leave in Europe

It was coming up to our leave time. We had to take 3 months leave every two years. For some reason we were not permitted to stay in Africa but had to go back to the U.K. I thought 3 months was an awful long time to be away from home with two small children.

Jeanette was a travel agent and had booked our sea trip via the East Coast to end up in Venice. That would use up quite a bit of time. Jane was three months and Tommy was about 15 months. We went by an Italian ship, the Europa of the Lloyd Triestino Company. We went by train to Durban to catch the boat and stayed with a cousin Esme Elliot. They took us to the docks and saw the ship off. There were some interesting people on board and we sat at a table with Justice Rumpff (later Chief Justice of South Africa) who apparently was well known in South Africa. I think he liked it that we had never heard of him. He was interesting and fun and we all got on well at the table. We had Italian food and every night they would produce something from a specific region. I am afraid I did not appreciate it at all as I felt so sea sick most of the time! Ian of course loved the food and the whole sea voyage was just down his street. I had to wash the babies' nappies every day in a little scullery place with sinks that you had to bend down to reach. The bending was terrible and I was very much regretting not having dear Ida to do it for me.

The sailors adored the babies and would come every day to see me on the deck and enquire about them. They would spend a long time just looking at them. They must have been very home sick. One evening we heard that the sailors were going on strike. The passengers had to serve the meals and do the washing up afterwards. I think even the cook was threatening to go on strike. Luckily the company persuaded the crew to go back to work as the passengers had made such a mess in the kitchen that the cook had complained!

Going this route to Europe via the Suez Canal is very interesting. We stopped at Dar es Salaam, where we had a few hours to look at the town. The next stop was Mombasa in Kenya. That was a longer stop and we took a taxi to a lovely beach. Then it was a visit to Mogadishu. The ship had to anchor in the roadstead, as there were no facilities on the docks for large vessels and we had to stay on board. There were no cranes on the docks at all. Ian had decided that when we stopped at Aden we would buy a camera. We went ashore as soon as we docked, took a taxi to a camera shop and bought an Asahi Pentax. I was thrilled to bits having only had a small box Brownie previously. I suppose one takes quite a chance buying expensive items at these tax havens as you could never get a warranty but that camera served me so well over the years. We had a good trip round Aden, rode on a camel (smelly thing) and saw our ship out in the roadstead from the top of the mountains. Again the ship had to anchor away from the shore and we went ashore and returned on a lighter. The next part of the trip was really hot, going through the Red Sea. We were all glad to reach Suez. Ian and I stayed on board while some of the other passengers took a taxi to Cairo and then to Port Said where we picked them all up again. We thought it would be a bit much with the babies. Those people missed going through the Suez Canal, which I would have been very sorry to miss. It was exciting. On one bend in the Canal we saw a few ships ahead of us and they looked as if they were sailing along on the desert. When we got to Port Said we were inundated with hawkers who tried to swarm the ship and sell us all kinds of things. Ian called them Gully Gully men. He had seen them on his trips to and from India as a child and then later on when he was in the army and went out to Hong Kong. He disliked them intensely!

It was starting to cool off now as we sailed across the Mediterranean and by the time we arrived at Trieste, which was the end of the sea voyage, it was really cold. We travelled to Venice and spent a few nights there in a hotel. I took lots of photos with my new camera and loved the walks that we did. We were slightly limited to what we could do because we had a very small baby with us and no pram but I still managed to get the feel of the place and loved it. I had heard some English people talking about there being a strike in France. We asked around and no one knew anything about a strike so we set off for Paris as we had planned. We arrived in Paris to find that there was indeed a strike and it was pretty extensive too. There was nothing going on at the Gare de Lyon. There was no hot water anywhere for my baby's bottles; no food to buy, no taxis running and we were wondering what we should do. Ian phoned the Embassy and pulled some strings and managed to get a car to take us to the Gare du Nord so that we could catch our next train to Calais. When we eventually arrived at Victoria Station I was exhausted and we just had to sleep the night at a hotel before going on to Bournemouth to Ian's father. Poor little Tommy was also exhausted and he badly needed a place to sleep comfortably. Jane being so much younger had not turned a hair. As long as she was fed and kept clean and dry she was very happy.

Ian's father lived in a small flat in Bournemouth with his housekeeper Helen Shanahan. We had to all fit in which we did and we spent quite a while there. My father in law had bought an enormous turkey for Christmas, which I had to cook in rather a small oven. That turkey lasted for so long! I tried everything to disguise it by currying it, putting in a cheesy white sauce and we still could not finish it! I think he thought the children would have huge appetites! Jane was only having milk and Tommy was a poor eater anyway!

We went to visit Ian's old friend Miss MacSymon in her beautiful little cottage on the New Forest called Godshill Wood cottage. She kept a tidy house and told me everything had a place and had to be kept in that place. Tommy one day spent a long time being very quiet and I discovered that he was carefully taking coal dust out of the coal bucket and carrying it across the room and putting it in a toy lorry. The trouble was he was using a sugar-sifting spoon with holes in it so there was a trail of coal dust wherever he had been! We also visited Ian's aunt Lily, his mother's sister in Calne in Wiltshire. She had worked in a sausage factory in Calne. She had a son called Neil who we did not meet.

My very dear Aunt Joan had agreed to look after the children for two weeks while Ian and I went skiing. Looking back on it I wonder how we had the cheek to ask her to do this! She had four of her own children but as far as we could make out her children absolutely loved having these small people in the house. We had a very good holiday in our favourite place Oberau and came back really refreshed. We had to kill a lot of time at Victoria station on the way back to Scotland so we sat in the cinema where it was warm. I was fiddling with my wedding ring, which fell off, and I heard it roll away under the chairs in front of us. We searched high and low but never found that ring. Ian was very upset with me " throwing away my wedding ring" and I was pretty upset too. I had it made to match a lovely gold bracelet that Ian gave me for my 21st birthday. Joan and Donald were happy to see us back safely and said they had loved having the babies. Certainly my cousins Pamela, Katherine, Jeffery and Louise had enjoyed it!

That was the end of our leave and we flew back to South Africa. I had needed to change Jane's nappy in Nairobi and had taken her into the ladies room. I put my bag down and when I left I forgot to pick it up again. The airhostess was handing round the immigration slips to fill in before we landed and I groped around for my bag. Oh my word! I knew exactly where it was! We asked the captain if he could radio back to ask someone to look out for the bag. He did that and told us it had been found and it would be on the next flight to Johannesburg. I worried all the way what we would do once we arrived with no passports or papers at all. The officials in Johannesburg were wonderful. They knew what had happened from the staff on the plane. All we had to do was say that we would come back to the airport to show the passports once my bag had arrived. In those days the department for immigration did not have a reputation for kindness or tolerance so we were expecting to have a very hard time. We were so surprised at the way we were treated, and very grateful.

7.   Back in Manzini, then Hlatikulu

I was pleased to be on familiar home ground again. Jane was also pleased to be out of her sleeping bag, which we had to use to keep her warm. She was so pleased to be out of it and wearing just a nappy. She lay on her stomach in my mother's garden kicking as much as she could. I think she grew much stronger with all that kicking.

It was soon time to set off for Manzini. I was not best pleased to go back to that house but decided I would make the best of it. Ian had wanted to join the Manzini club but there was a row going on which he did not want to get involved in. So we did not play tennis, nor could we swim which I regretted.

There was a guava plantation next door to our house and Benson used to go in and pick me as many as we needed. The plantation did not seem to belong to anyone so I never felt I was actually stealing. I thought they were all volunteer trees. I used to make guava jelly and guava juice which the children never liked much.

I was now expecting my third baby and was starting to feel a bit sick as usual. This time it was not as bad so I thought it was most likely another boy. I had some check ups at the Raleigh Fitkin hospital and all was going well. I was so grateful to have that hospital nearby and did not have to go to the one in Mbabane!

One day I had been up the road to have tea with Sheena in the afternoon and on the way home I overtook a large flatbed lorry carrying a bulldozer. It was creeping down the hill towards the circle near our house. I got home, took the children into the house and heard the most almighty crash. The whole town heard it and we all dashed out to see what had happened. The truck had lost control, the brakes had failed and it had gone straight across the circle and landed upside down in my garden. It hit the garage and the gate and fence. It was such a terrible accident and I was shaking like a leaf. I had just been right in the path of that truck five minutes before it happened. The driver had jumped out and was nowhere to be seen. His co driver was under the truck in my garden the poor man. Errol Reck, the local hotel owner came running down to make sure that I was alright and he telephoned Ian and told him to come home. Ian had heard the noise of crash and had not thought it could possibly be in our garden. He came straight home and dealt with the aftermath of the accident. It took me a while to be able to go outside into the garden and we played on the other side of the house if we did go outside. I was also hoping that the next baby would not have been affected at all. Errol had also thought about that when he came running to help me. It was a dreadful experience and I was very shaken.

A few weeks later Ian came home with that special look on his face, which I had been waiting for and hoping would happen soon! We were to be transferred to Hlatikulu. Ian was to be District Commissioner. I had heard about this town and knew that it was a lovely place so I looked forward to the move very much. Just to get away from that house was enough to get me excited. Ian's colleague Peter Simkin had been based there and had really liked it very much. So we had an idea of what was coming.

The house in Hlatikulu was lovely. It was an old Colonial style house with a deep verandah all round and set in a large garden with sweeping lawns and wonderful old trees. One of the trees was the biggest Poinsettia I had ever seen. All the bedrooms led out to the verandah. There had been an addition quite recently and a whole guest wing had been built with two bedrooms and a bathroom. So we knew we would be able to have lots of guests to visit us! None of our previous houses had enough space really for visitors.

The lorry that brought our possessions was of course far bigger than the previous one but it managed to negotiate the steep roads to Hlatikulu. There were a couple of rivers to cross as well as mountain passes between Manzini and Hlatikulu. The countryside was beautiful and we were thrilled to see the different type of landscapes. We heard there was a deep gorge called Grand Valley, which we knew we would be visiting as soon as we could.

I had to make my name known at the hospital for my ante natal check ups and was pleased to see that I had a Doctor K. who I knew was a political refugee from South Africa. He was very caring and good and I was happy that I would not be having the same doctor I had the misfortune to have in Mbabane for Tom's delivery. Or so I thought!

This house was a total delight. There were 4 bedrooms, two bathrooms, a big kitchen with an old wood stove. It had a walk in pantry with one of those marble tabletops to keep things cool as well as a lot of shelves. Obviously designed for entertaining large numbers of people! We were always issued with standard Government furniture, which was adequate but dull and would be seen in all the officers' houses. To make our house different I tried to brighten things up with rugs and cushions that I had made.

The previous occupants of our house used to keep some geese and chickens. He was on leave and had not been able to get the birds to his mother in-law so he asked if he could leave them until he was back from leave. I did not mind at all until I found out what horrid vicious birds geese are! They hissed at me every time I went outside the back door. The only one of us who was not afraid of them was Jane. She was about the same size as them but had absolutely no fear of them. I had to go out armed with a big stick before they would let me out!

It was here that I started making hooked rugs for the floor and patchwork quilts for the children's beds. In those days I just used the old fabric that I had from dressmaking. I also scrounged bits and pieces off all my friends and family. I had seen a "Grandmothers Garden" pattern once and decided to use that hexagon pattern over cardboard. I used old Corn Flake packets for that. I was also busy making clothes for us all. There were no shops for clothes really in Swaziland in those days. I made all our clothes. I had to buy the fabric whenever I had a chance, either in Johannesburg or Piet Retief which was our nearest big town in South Africa. That was where we went to the dentist and I decided that I would do a three-month shop there when we would squeeze the entire shopping, dentist, and anything else we needed into a one day outing.

The shops in Hlatikulu were a village store, a vegetable table run by local women and not much else. I could see that we needed to grow our own vegetables again so started on that project as soon as I could. The women at the stall sold some little vegetables called sousous. They grew very easily on a vine but we all disliked them intensely. I tried to doctor them with cheese sauce, curry sauce and all manner of other ingenious things but they really were nasty. They had such a horrible texture. I was glad when sousou season was over. I hired a full time gardener called Zephania and his wife who was to help look after the children. He was not allowed to plant sousous! His wife proved to be rather a bad choice of child minder, as she would tell them very scary stories and frighten them.

My friend Angela Kurnot (Previously Lemon) came to visit us in Hlatikulu with her three sons. It was such fun having her there and she loved the area. She badly needed to get away from her husband for a while. Unfortunately while she was with us Cyclone Claude hit Swaziland. Well it was actually the tail end of the cyclone luckily but it was enough to cause havoc. I have never seen so much rain before. We were completely marooned and Angela could not have got home even if she had taken a chance. The roads became impassable. My big worry with all these people in the house was the food supply. The lorries that normally brought our food could not get through and we were essentially cut off from anywhere. Luckily my friend Pat Jameson (the policeman Dave's wife) was away in Mbabane and she told me to raid her pantry until I could get supplies.

There was a pub in the village run by a Frenchman called Bob Sole. There was also a very good tennis club, which we joined. Some of the local farmers would come and play every Saturday so there would usually be a bit of a party afterwards. There were two brothers who were rival tennis players, Robin and Oliver Hall. We saw a lot of Oliver Hall and his wife Maureen. They had a farm in Hluti and they grew Granadillas. They were very welcoming to us and we visited their farm often. Ian had to drive through Hluti on the way down to his court circuit in Golela and he would drop in on the policeman stationed there. One day he noticed that the flag was flying at half-mast so he asked who had died. He was told "Little Piddle" had died - his little dog. He said luckily "Big Piddle" did not die! Hluti is far enough away from the powers that be for him to get away with this! It would not have been tolerated in Manzini or Mbabane!

The sad demise of Little Piddle

The other people in the village that we would make good friends with were Colonel Frank Loringh Van Beeck and his delightful wife Netty. He had been in the Dutch free army in WW2 and had previously been a cavalry officer and formally ADC to Queen Juliana. He was 47 when war broke out, went over to the U.K and was trained in parachuting in Scotland so that they could use him to get behind the enemy lines. Coming from Holland he was familiar with the country. He did land behind enemy lines in Holland and had the distinct advantage of knowing all the good hiding places in his town. He told us he pushed his grandmother's coffin up in the crypt where they were hiding and told her he needed the space for his men!

Next door to Netty and the Colonel was Brigadier Hartshorn Hill, nicknamed Scrubbs (Hartshorn is the name for Scrubbs ammonia). He had been in the South African army during the First World War, lost one arm at Gallipoli (catching a grenade which would have killed them all and throwing it out of the trench). When WW2 broke out he volunteered for service and was told they did not take disabled people. "Me disabled? What are you saying? I can shoot better than anyone in this room." They gave him a gun and sent up some clay pigeons and he shot them all down. So he was back in the army. He and the Colonel used to swap stories of their wartime experiences. I am just so sorry that Netty and I would tune out half the time and neither of us wrote down these reminiscences. I remember scraps of the stories only. He served in the army "up north" as he would say. He wrote a book about his experiences called Avenge Tobruk. He and the Colonel would have the odd spat, usually when one felt the other had insulted him in some way. They would not speak to each other for a while but eventually they would start up their conversations again. Scrubbs sometimes went on the water wagon as he would put it and then he became a real bore - we wanted him back on his gin. That was far more interesting. He drank Gordon's Gin and the Colonel drank Geneva (Dutch gin) and they even argued over that!

Netty was a well-known portrait painter. She painted under the name of Netty Franken and had commissions from all over Europe. She had met Frank at the end of the war when the regiment that Frank was serving in had liberated her town. He was the commanding officer and the town council commissioned Netty to paint a portrait of the man who had liberated their town. She fell in love with him during his sittings and she came back to South Africa with him to live in Hlatikulu. The portrait hangs in the council chambers in Bergen Op Zoom in Holland. He was still married to his wife and being a good Catholic the colonel could not divorce her, so she lived on their farm outside Swaziland and he lived with Netty in an attractive old house looking out over the bush. When his wife died one of Ian's colleagues, Peter Simkin, married them much to our surprise because we had all assumed that they were a married couple. They had one son also called Frank. Netty painted a portrait of Tommy while we were in Hlatikulu. She said she liked to paint children when they were about three. They still had the baby face but had developed their own personality. She certainly caught Tommy extremely well. She went on to paint all of us eventually. The children called him Colonel Peppermint because he always gave them a peppermint when he saw them. They adored him!

The policeman in Hlatikulu was Dave Jameson. His wife Pat had a son older than our children. She was a good friend and helped me settle into this new place. She knew all the other police wives that I had been friends with. Our garden had an enormous plum tree in the vegetable patch. The local children knew exactly when they would be ripe and would hang around asking if they could have some. There were so many on the tree I had no problems sharing them. Benson used to go off with a Rand or two and come home with lovely fresh mealies for us to eat. He bought them from locals who grew them in their gardens. Mine never seemed to get that big! There were some beautiful plants in our garden. Someone must have been a great gardener when she lived there. Outside the gate was a patch of lovely little pink arum lilies which were indigenous and we never saw them anywhere else at all.

Benson had settled into his new school and Ida was happy to

be in Hlatikulu as that was her home ground. She had to attend various ceremonies and so we got to see her in her lovely tribal outfit. She was very impressive with her hair stacked up into a huge headdress, her long beaded skirt and her beads and other ornaments around her neck.

Not one of the doors in this house had a key so I could never lock anything up safely. It did not really worry me much until I heard that there had been a mass escape from the prison. The little lane at the back of our house led to the Police Lines and then after that there was the prison. So it was pretty close to the house. I had to admit that I was nervous until they had the prisoners back inside again. Ian used to be away for days at a time when he had to go to Golela to take court. Golela was in the south of his District and he drove down every six weeks or so. Golela was just on the South African border. In fact the tennis court was in both countries. So you played one half of the game in Swaziland and the other in South Africa. The pub was on the Swaziland side and so the South Africans would buy their beers through the tennis club fence so as to avoid the draconian drink laws on the other side.

He always took his shotgun with him when he went down to Golela in case he saw some guinea fowl to shoot. He only ever shot one and I refused to deal with it so he never did that again. On his way back he would stop at a butchery on the side of the road to buy us some fillet steak. He always had to show the butcher which bit he wanted. They did not set any extra price on fillet, as they saw no advantage in having it, so it was incredibly cheap. I thought it would be quite safe to eat it as long as I cooked it! I certainly had no other access to fresh meat in the village. I used to buy in bulk in Piet Retief and freeze it in packs.

We were given a small brown puppy of dubious origin who we called Lola. So Scratch had a companion and the children had a new puppy to play with. She was a stupid dog and almost untrainable so was to become an outside dog. The children loved the garden and were very happy in Hlatikulu. My sister Ellen and her children came out to see us while they were based in Brunei. She sailed from Singapore to Lourenco Marques (now Maputo). We drove down, met them off the boat, and came back in one day. My mother also came to see Ellen and she drove them up to Johannesburg when they had been with us for a few days. It was lovely to have the children. We had seen Mark and Chris in England but Kate was new to us. She was a shy little girl and very sweet. I had a swing in the garden and they had fun on that. We had great fun with them and had some picnics in Grand Valley, which everyone thought was a fabulous place. It was close to us and we could get there easily as long as it had not rained recently. The track down got pretty difficult if it was wet. The valley had a fast flowing river in it, a grassy area where we would have our picnic, and lovely big trees. We often saw cattle there and once watched a herdsman taking a whole string of cattle across the river to graze on the other side. I think there had once been a scheme to grow rice along the riverbanks but nothing came of it. There was always water in that river so it might have worked. We used to go in the land rover as the track could be very tricky in places. Unfortunately all the rivers in Swaziland had bilharzia in them so we had to be vigilant in keeping the children well away from the water. They always wanted to play in the water. We had some great braais down in Grand Valley with friends.

We had no electricity in Hlatikulu but there was a generator, which gave us light in the evening. So Ida was back to hand washing and I had to learn how to start the generator when Ian was away. I did not mind starting it but I was very afraid to go outside in the pitch dark to turn it off. Ian rigged up a wire from the outside shed to a string that hung above the bed which I could pull to switch the generator off. That was a great improvement for me! Of course we were back to lanterns and Tilly Lamps and all that goes with them. It had to be a daily routine to clean the glasses, trim the wicks and fill the lamps - something that we had been taking for granted when we had electricity in Manzini. I converted my sewing machine back to hand operated as well so that I could continue with my sewing. The ironing was done with one of those really heavy cast iron ones, which you put on the top of the stove to get hot. When it was hot you lifted it up with a towel and did the ironing. Ian had to be in his "ice cream suit" for the queen's birthday parade and poor Ida could not get it looking smart. Every time she ironed it a smut streaked across it and she would have to start all over again. Ian felt so sorry for her that he bought a gas iron, which was far easier to handle.

One time when I had to entertain some people from Mbabane, I had prepared fillet steak as beef olives, wrapped in bacon and all held together with toothpicks. I put this dish in the pantry to wait unto the time came to cook it and went in later to check on something. The cat had found the dish and had eaten at least half of the little rolls of fillet. I had to dash up to the butcher and persuade him to sell me something that would be good enough for these guests! I could have easily killed that cat! After that I always had a back up plan!

Jane had made a friend in Hlatikulu. He was an old tramp that often sat on the steps outside the shop eating bread and jam. Jane thought he was wonderful and would climb into his lap and cuddle up against him. He was harmless but I did keep an eye on her all the time. Apparently he inherited a large sum on money from a distant relative and when the policeman went to tell him about this he said he did not want it. Money just brings trouble and he didn't want any trouble!

We had several remittance men in Swaziland, people of "good family name" who were paid by their families to keep out of England. One was Oliver Tetley who was an amiable man full of bonhomie and liked by everyone. His family kept him in the style to which he was accustomed but he did run out of funds sometimes. During one of the visits of one of the bigwigs (I forget who it was) Oliver tried to gate crash the party. The policeman at the door tried to tell him to go away but the important person's wife recognised him and called him over saying "Oliver Darling how wonderful to see you". It turned out she was his godmother.

Child care with the local tramp

I was hoping to deliver the new baby without having to wait out the extra three weeks like my previous babies. So Ian took me down to Grand Valley. This was an extremely bumpy trip in the Land Rover over steep roads but it did nothing to induce this child to be born! I had to just wait. My pregnancy was advancing and I was due at the end of January. It was quite warm and humid at that time of year. The hospital was just up the road and I was looking forward to being back to normal. The Government hospital there was very big as it had a large catchment area. I was the only white patient when I went in to have the baby. As usual I had to have an induction and Dr Kaplan assured me he would be with me when the baby was born. Everything was going well and I had advanced nicely with the delivery and suddenly all contractions stopped and nothing was happening. I begged Dr Kaplan to give me one more injection, as I was sure the baby would be born soon. He eventually gave in (I think against his better judgement) and did it and then went off to hold his clinic. I knew straight away that the baby was going to be born any minute and called out for him. The doctor's room was next door to mine and in came the doctor that I had done everything I could to avoid ever seeing again. She had a cigarette dangling out her mouth. She washed her hands quickly, put the cigarette out and delivered Robert. I was very fed up with Dr Kaplan for leaving me like that. It had all been a most public birth with all and sundry looking in on me all day long. Robert was bundled up in a cloth and put in a little wooden box right next to the autoclave just in case he should get cold! It was mid summer and terribly hot so I insisted on having him next to my bed instead of in that hot place. They thought I was very odd.

Unfortunately another patient had been admitted the day after Robert was born. He had the DTs and could never remember which was his ward. He tried to get into my bed one night and that was when I lost it and the doctor was told to discharge him until I went home. His wife had to cope with him for a few days. The matron used to come and see me every day to see how I was doing. She and I would discuss what we (the only two white people in the hospital) would have for our meals. She clearly had no idea of how the shops worked and would decide on chops one day. She did not know that chops only come in on one day of the week and not that particular day. We had a good laugh over that.

As soon as Robert was born I asked the sister to run and telephone my husband to let him know the good news as it was nearly a quarter to five and I knew the telephone exchange would close at quarter to five. She ran off and gave Ian the message. A woman called Gertie Van Der Vyver ran the exchange. She knew exactly what was going on in the village and she knew where we were most of the time! So she would have heard the news too! Gerty had a spat with Bob Sole's wife over something and they ended up squabbling in the street using an umbrella as a weapon.

My mother had come down to help us at home while I was in hospital. She had a terrible drive down in pouring rain and had trouble slipping about in the thick Swaziland mud. But she was made of stern stuff and managed to get through all right. She brought the two other children to the hospital to meet the new baby and was horrified at the conditions in the hospital. She had to walk through the casualty on her way and then when she got to me the children climbed on my bed having just been through all that filth. She said to me "if this baby survives this he will survive anything!" He was a survivor and was another easy baby. It was fun bringing him home and I could see that he would be no trouble.

Ian's Uncle Teddy came out to see us just after Robert was born. He loved the place and said it reminded him so much of his time in Malaya. He stayed about 6 weeks which felt like quite a long time. Ian took him away on a holiday to the

Drakensberg and the children and I went to stay with an old school friend in Natal, Helen Mousley (Lindsay).

I had been troubled by my wisdom teeth and the dentist in Piet Retief had told me that as soon as the baby was born I ought to have them out. So one day Ida, the baby in her arms Tommy, Jane and I set out for Piet Retief. I had the extraction done and drove home bleeding quite a lot. The teeth had been terribly infected and I had a raging fever by the time I got home. The doctor had to come out urgently to me as I was so ill. Doctors normally did not do house calls but when he heard what I had just had done he came very quickly. He gave me an injection and pills to take and that sorted me out. Not a pleasant experience. While we were at the dentist he noticed Jane sucking her thumb and had a quick look at her mouth. He told me if I did not want to have expensive orthodontic treatment in the future I should do my best to stop her sucking her thumb as she was altering her mouth alignment. I could see what he meant but it was very hard to stop her. Nasty aloe ointment painted onto her nails didn't seem to stop her. One time when I had been to the dentist in Piet Retief I came upon a most terrible accident. A flock of sheep, which was being driven to another farm, was mown down by a huge logging truck, which overturned on a corner. I got there just after it had happened and was very distressed to see the poor animals. I helped the driver out of the truck and took him to the police station and begged the police to hurry up and go with guns to put them out of their misery. I could not eat lamb again for a long time after seeing that.

While we lived in Hlatikulu, John Sturgis had his magisterial visits. He would have lunch with us every time he came. It was expected of me to do this and sometimes was not really convenient. He could only just tolerate the children but he always enjoyed Ian's company.

8.   Goedgegun (now Nhlangano)

Ian had an unexpected change in his work situation and the main office was now to be in Goedgegun instead of at Hlatikulu. They had actually told him he had to move soon after we had arrived in Hlatikulu and having just unpacked all those boxes I refused point blank to do it all over again. It was the only time I became "difficult" over a move! So Ian had to commute to the office down the hill at Goedgegun until I was prepared to move again which would be after this baby was born and settled. He was behind me in this and thought it very unreasonable to expect us to move once again about 6 weeks after arriving. So we were lucky to have as long as we did in that lovely house. Yes it was time to pack up again and move into a small unassuming little house in Goedgegun, which did not seem to have much to recommend it! Robert must have been about two months when we moved.

Our immediate neighbours in Goedgegun were the Badenhorsts. He was in the veterinary department and she took me under her wing. She saw that I needed a bit of mothering after the move! She had a hedge of Amatungulas in her garden and she showed me how to make the most delicious jelly out of them. I had eaten them before on the Natal coast but had never seen them again. She grew lots of vegetables and she was so generous with them that I hardly needed to bother with growing any of our own. My garden was pretty dull anyway so I did not bother with making it look better as I had heard we would get a better house soon. Goedgegun was bigger than Hlatikulu with a much larger population of working people. It had more shops and things going on. Of course there was a club, which became the hub of activities. There was a wonderful family called McSephany who were the mainstays at parties or socials. They had a shop in town. There was another family called Language. August Language was a lawyer and a character of note. There was a story that the judge once asked his clerk "who is that noisy bugger?", to which his clerk naturally replied "Language, m'lud". A new Dominee (priest) was brought in to the Dutch Reformed Church. I think he was the first one they ever had. They built him a house, filled the pantry up, furnished it and made him and his new wife welcome. I rather envied her introduction into the community. I could have done with some of that support at times! The other character we met and liked very much was Oom Ben. He was the owner of the local chemist shop. His name was Ben Esterhuizen and a family member, (I think his father), was the Director of Education. It was his son Richard E Grant who directed the film called Wah-Wah. We saw the film in Port Elizabeth much later on when it came out. It was set in Swaziland in the 1960s so we really enjoyed seeing all the familiar places, but Ian was irritated by its lack of accuracy about the administration and protocol during the independence celebrations!

This little house we had been allocated was only a stepping-stone. The Government had bought a better larger house for the District Commissioner to live in. We just had to wait while the PWD did some alterations. I was allowed to choose my type of cooker and I chose to have a Raeburn which was an anthracite burning one. I had got used to the wood burning one in Hlatikulu and did not want a gas stove. I think they thought I was mad asking for that. We knew that there was a coal mine not far away and it would always be easy to get coal. We had quite a wait for that house so I had to make the best of it once again and make a happy home for the family. Not easy when you know that you are moving soon.

Ian's father came to stay with us while we were in that house. I fetched him at Hluhluwe game reserve in Natal. I left Robert in Ida's capable hands. He was on a bottle by then and I knew she would cope with the other two while I was away. The drive took me about 5 hours and when I arrived Stanley was so relieved to see me. I think he thought he had been abandoned in darkest Africa, not knowing a soul and not sure about anything, he was quite rightly worried stiff. I could see how confused he was and realized very soon that he should never have been allowed to travel such a distance. He was a bit too fond of his gin and by the time I got there had had quiet a few. I had to help him to his room and wondered how I was going to cope with him and the children at home. We spent an extra night there so that I could show him the wild life and to give me a rest from the long distance driving. We drove back to Goedgegun and I was happy to see my children again.

Grandpa settled himself into a routine. He taught Ida how to pour his gin and angostura bitters. He disliked going to braais and we would often leave him behind if we went out. But that was also a problem, as he would worry all the time that we might not come back. He became more and more confused. It was becoming a real worry, as he would go off to post a letter in the post box. Since we did not have a postal service that was problematic. I had to get the staff to go out and look for him wandering about looking for the post box. All the local staff were alert to the problem and they helped him home when he was lost. Unfortunately he became ill with a kidney infection. I nursed him as well as I could until I went down with the same infection and could not nurse him any more. They took him away in an ambulance to the Hlatikulu hospital where he sadly died a few weeks later. He is buried in the churchyard in Hlatikulu, which is a beautiful spot, and I know he would have been happy to know he was in such a nice place. It was at this time that I really was aware of what an extraordinary community we lived in. August Language's wife Taffy came and took the children off while we dealt with the funeral. I had not even met her. Everyone was extremely kind and most especially as I was quite ill myself.

We had a broken windscreen and the only place we could get it replaced was in Manzini so I set off to do that. The road wound downhill very steeply and was pretty slippery, as it had been raining hard. I managed alright peering through the little hole Ian had made for me. He did not want to take the whole windscreen out in case it rained on the way. I made it to Manzini and left the car in the glass works place. I stayed with Harry and Sheena Shirley but I very soon realized that my kidney infection was back badly and I was running a high temperature. They put me to bed and I fetched the car in the morning and drove back home by which time I was really ill. Once again the doctor had to come out to me to do a home visit. His bad luck was that he was very drunk (which Ian noticed) He gave me treatment and went on his way but the next day Ian reported him for being drunk on duty and he was dismissed.

Our house was at long last ready for us to move into. It was a very unusual house in that it had been built in two sections quite separate from each other. The lower half was where the bedrooms and bathroom were and the other upper part was where there was a large sitting room, dining room, kitchen and scullery. It had a nice big verandah which looked out over the garden. The garden was well established and interesting. The previous owner was a Mr Van Heerden who had collected as many of the indigenous aloes he could get hold of. He also collected proteas and silver leaf trees and amazingly they did incredibly well there. So we had a really beautiful garden. It was very big and took a lot of upkeep but I loved it. There was a big vegetable patch and the ground was fertile and well composted. We were never short of lovely fresh vegetables there. There was a small white Stinkwood tree which gave just enough shade for the pram and a spot for us to sit in the shade and play.

I was not all that keen on going outside at night to go to bed so I built a walk way for us. I bought some breeze bricks and laid them by myself till I reached roof height. Then I got a Swazi to make a thatch roof for my walkway. I had never done any building before and I probably did not make the mixtures quite right. It sagged slightly in the middle but it served its purpose. You can't take a baby outside in the pouring rain to go to bed. Luckily this house had keys, which I used when Ian was away on his court circuit. One night I heard someone rattling all the door handles. Ian had taken our shotgun in case he saw a guinea fowl. The only other weapon I had was his old fishing speargun. I lay in bed clutching the speargun and was quite prepared to fire a nasty arrow at the burglar. I was lucky that night as the burglar broke in two doors down the road from our house. It was the only attempt at burglary that I had while we were there.

When Robert was about three months I went down with measles. I knew I was pretty sick but could not diagnose myself so I drove up to Hlatikulu to see the doctor. He took one look and made the diagnosis. Its not at all funny getting childhood diseases when you are an adult. I was a very sick person for a few days. Ida had to cope all on her own with the children. She was such a brilliant person and just took it all in her stride. I did not let the children near me and they did not catch it. I could not bear any light and lay in a darkened room for what seemed like a long time.

One of our friends the Wynns who lived in Mankayane gave us a dear little Pointer puppy who we called Scramble. He was an easy dog to train and fitted in perfectly. Scratch accepted him without a murmur. He was quite boisterous like all puppies but soon became acceptable. Ian loved taking the three dogs for long walks and we had found some really good places to go to for walks. I always looked out on these walks for the dead heads of the wild flowers at the end of summer so that I could make a huge arrangement of dead flower heads. There were some marvellously different ones, the Watsonias being the best of all. There was such a variety that the arrangement looked very good. Ian used to tell me to throw it away at the end of winter because it was collecting dust!

At about this time we had a visit from what Ian called a "visiting fireman." Politicians used to come out to Swaziland to have a look and as Ian said to spend some of the taxpayers money. They never achieved anything so it seemed. This one was Mr. John Stonehouse and he was the rudest guest I have ever had. As he walked in the door he gave me a list of things he wanted for breakfast most of which I did not have in the house and told him so. We had sent the children to a friend so that he did not see them at all. I was infuriated when I heard later that he complained about my badly behaved children (who he had never even seen!) One thing he demanded was an airmail letter. I did not have one in the house but managed to borrow one from a friend who nearly did not let me have it when she heard whom it was for! He then wrote his letter and made me go and post it. I told him it would not go until tomorrow afternoon anyway and could just as well be posted in the morning but he couldn't believe that we did not have a postal service in the evening and so I had to go. Years later it turned out that he was a spy in the pay of the Czechs.

We had to have a cocktail party for him and all the dignitaries of the town. There were some that I would have preferred not to invite to my house but we had to do it. I had special treatment for them. I had found some tins of delicious French smoked frogs' legs at the Indians' store and I would serve them on little biscuits. Some people never came back to my house after that!

While we were in the South of Swaziland Ian had to go to Mbabane for meetings. The route took you through Mankayana where there was a pub. Quite an elderly woman who had an interesting history ran this. She had been a pilot in the war flying the planes that needed to be flown back after repair. She ran a tight ship at the pub and did not stand any nonsense. We met a nice young couple that farmed near Mankayana and visited them often when we had to go through. They asked me to invigilate the Matric exams at the

An evening with the badly behaved Butler children

local school which I did one year. The school had a corrugated iron roof, which made a very loud thundering noise one day when we had a hailstorm right in the middle of the exams. The school was really fussy about the boys' clothes and I had to refuse one boy access to the classroom until he was properly dressed for the exam. I thought that was a bit harsh, as I knew he would fail the exam if he did not get back to school in time.

Robert was a delightful baby but he got up to a fair amount of mischief. Even as a very young baby he knew how to have fun. He decorated his cot with the contents of his nappy one day when he was bored with his afternoon sleep. We had to take the cot and the baby outside and hose them down to get them cleaned up! He loved mangoes and I would take all his clothes off and leave him outside in the garden to eat his mango. We used to hose him down after that and he loved it! He would laugh and really enjoyed being squirted with water!

My Aunt Cecil, her husband Jumbo and some of their daughters came down to see us in Goedgegun. They were very interested in our garden and spent hours identifying all the aloes and proteas. Grand Valley was still close enough to go to from there so we took them for a drive there too. We also had visits from Guy and Anne Berry who were keen to see the garden. Guy had been our family doctor when we were children and they were great friends of my parents. By the time all these really knowledgeable people had been I knew all the names of most of my plants. I was infuriated when all the names changed later on for scientific clarity! I bought or was given a few good books on the plants and was fortunate to inherit from my Grandfather Smith, the Reynolds Aloe book. I developed an interest in the trees of Swaziland too and had started taking photographs of as many as I could identify. There are a few different Erythrynas, which I had seen in Stegi, Manzini and in the lowveld. Swaziland has a wonderful range of climates, topography and so boasts a large collection of different species.

9. Overseas leave again

In September of 1967 we went on overseas leave with all the children. Robert was about 18 months when we left. We sailed on a Dutch boat of the Holland Africa line and the children were cared for in the nursery if Ian and I wanted to play deck games or have time away from them. That was a first for us. The previous Italian boat did not have a nursery and we had to keep them with us all the time. So we made the most of it! We had booked ourselves in with Florian Sollerer in Oberau for a six week stay and were looking forward to having lots of walks in the mountains.

Ian was playing deck quoits one day and fell down. He said it felt as if someone had kicked him in the Achilles tendon. He turned round to see who had done it and could not take any weight on his leg at all. He had torn the tendon and he was unable to walk at all. There were three doctors on the boat and not one of them knew anything much about Orthopedics. I could see that the tendon was not intact and eventually persuaded the doctors to put his leg in a plaster of Paris so that at least he would be able to walk with crutches. It was a very difficult journey from Amsterdam with three small children, a husband on crutches and me coping with the entire luggage. As soon as we arrived in Oberau he went to see the local doctor who diagnosed immediately what was wrong. It's a common skiing injury so he was familiar with it. Ian was admitted into the hospital in Worgl and the tendon was repaired with a zed plasty. I was in the house with Florian and Peppi unable to speak any German but learned very soon how to ask for the washing machine, the kitchen and everything I needed! I used to get a lift with the policeman every day so that I could go and see Ian. His name was Sepp and it was kind of him to take me as I don't think he was really supposed to do things like that. Luckily he had to report to headquarters every day so I got to see Ian. The hospital was run by nuns and he was well looked after. The doctor who did the operation told me he did so many each year that he could do it in his sleep!

While Ian was in hospital I noticed that Robert's face was swollen just under his jaw. I took him to see the doctor and was told he had Mumps. This was pretty awkward as we were eating our lunches at the Kellerwirt and I knew the organiser of the tours would not be best pleased to see me there with a mumpy child. I had an altercation with her but in the end she just told her guests to keep away from me! There was a nice little Welsh girl who Jane had been playing with and I wondered if she went down with mumps when she got home. Jane was very indignant with this child because she would not do things she asked her to do. I worked out the child could only speak Welsh and simply did not understand Jane!

Ian came out of hospital after about 10 days. He was to be in plaster for 6 weeks which meant the whole time we were in Oberau. He was very frustrated but we did do some short walks. He sent me off on a couple of bus trips when he realised I had had enough of things! I went with Florian who was a tour leader on the buses. We visited Stertzing in Italy and I remember going over the Brenner Pass, which was very impressive. Florian was great company. Because he was the leader of the tour, he was not allowed to buy wine in Italy, so I did it for him and sneaked the wine onto the bus for him. He said it was much cheaper than Austrian wine and I thought it was a good deal better too! I had a lovely Italian meal in a small café in the square. It was a lovely outing for me.

While we were in Austria a friend of mine Fredericka came to spend some time with us. She was an anaesthetist in Munich and I met her when I went on a British Council trip to Orkney and Shetland. She was very keen on collecting wild mushrooms, which she dried on the stoep at Florian's house. She found lots of different ones and knew their names and knew that they were not poisonous. She showed me the very best way of drying the baby's nappies on the line and her way really worked well.

When our six weeks were up in Austria we went over to England to stay with Uncle Teddy. Ian had heard that he had to give evidence in a murder trial in Swaziland and because it was in the middle of our leave they flew him back to South Africa specially. He had just come out of plaster so had a marginally better flight than if he had still been in plaster. He gave his evidence and came back to England. I was left with Uncle Teddy and the children. I am afraid I annoyed him rather by buying some delicious looking kippers I saw in the fish shop for breakfast. He seemed to think I had no right to make a contribution to the household! I was very glad to see Ian back again.

During this leave we also went to see Ian's old Aunt Lily who lived in Calne in Wiltshire. The children remembered that visit well because Robert tore the tablecloth she had put on the tea table and caused a rumpus! We also stayed with Miss MacSymon in the New Forest.

We sailed back to South Africa on a single class Union Castle boat called the Cape Town Castle. One of my cousins Mary Elliot was also on the boat so we saw her quite a bit during the voyage. One evening I was taking the children to supper when I accidentally closed Robert's little finger in the door. I had told the children to mind their fingers but I had not looked behind me. Robert had his finger in the hinge. Those doors to the cabin have a very watertight fit and his finger was badly crushed. It was terrible and the poor little boy was screaming with pain. I was trying to get someone to find Ian to look after the other two while I took him to the doctor. We could not find Ian so we all trooped in. The doctor strapped his two fingers together after stitching the gaping wound. He told me to keep it dry and have the stitches out when we docked in Cape Town. Well anyone trying to keep an 18 month old's finger dry can just try! It was very sweet when we got into the dining room eventually; with his finger all bandaged up he kept showing it to everyone saying "My Nini" he was so proud of it! I felt terrible but I knew I had said to them "mind your fingers"!

10. Manzini - again!

We had known before we left on leave that we would be moving to Manzini so once again we packed up the house in Goedgegun and moved down to the Lowveld. This time Ian was the District Commissioner and we had the lovely big house in a huge garden. It was just along the road from the other house we had lived in the last time we were in Manzini. I had walked past it on my way to town when he lived along the road and envied the people living there so now it was our house and I was thrilled! There was a large enclosed verandah. Well the closure was mosquito netting, so we could sleep out on the verandah if it was very hot.

This was a whole new time in the service for me. I was now the wife of the district commissioner and I automatically became Chairlady of the Red Cross Society. With that came a big load of responsibility. We ran a clinic for babies and mothers. I had been helping at the clinics previously but now it was all mine. I had some marvellous members on my committee. The two I remember most fondly were the two Pybus sisters. One of them had recognised me from having been the midwife to my mother during my birth. Apparently I look sufficiently like my mother for her to know exactly who I was! They lived on a small farm outside Manzini and were a tough old pair of women. They were great value in all our work. I crossed them one time when I organised a street collection on a certain day only to find that was Ash Wednesday and we could not possibly have a collection on that day! We also ran a soup kitchen and made huge pots of soup, which we would take up to the clinic. The mothers would bring a container to take the soup home. We bought powdered milk in large quantities and repacked it to sell at a very much-reduced price for the mothers. We also tried to teach basic hygiene methods in the bottle-feeding but I had my doubts about them being implemented as most of the folk who came in probably did not have running water nearby.

There was a lot of poverty and hunger in Swaziland and we tried our best to help. The clinics were fun as we got to know the regular mothers and their babies. We weighed the babies and gave advice on breast or bottle-feeding.

I was also expected to do a fair amount of entertaining. Now that I had the space this was easy. I think I was better at it by now too so managed it all more easily. Our staff had increased, and now we had Zephania in the garden and his wife helping Ida in the house. One day I spotted Zephenia outside our garden selling hard boiled eggs to the people passing by. I presumed they were the eggs from the neighbours' hens! He was supplementing his income. They were not an easy couple as the wife kept practising her witchcraft to make Ida leave our employment. So we had to part company even though he was such a good gardener.

As part of his job as DC, Ian had to marry people. I only realised that when one day a woman told me Ian had married her! I asked him about it and he said yes he had married her the month before. One day Liz and Ted Reilly came in one day and asked him to marry them. They had been living together for years and much to everyone's surprise they suddenly wanted to legalise it. Ian went through the usual questions and when he asked them if they had a ring they had not thought of that and they grabbed a paper clip and straitened it out and made a ring out of that. The whole thing was really unromantic but typical of that couple.

That year (1967) we had Christmas at home instead of going away to Lesotho or my parents in Johannesburg. My two younger brothers came and one of them, Robert, brought his girl friend who he was later to marry. It was very hot in Manzini at that time of year but we did not seem to notice. The two boys and Val went off to Mozambique to have a look there. I heard about that trip much later. It was probably the first time they had been away to somewhere like Mozambique

Ian had to marry a lot of people

without parental supervision! The younger brother Terry told me later that he did not like playing "gooseberry" very much!

There was a small pool in the garden, which did not have any sort of filter plant so we had to just empty it out and refill it when we thought it was too green. The children loved it and did not mind the colour of the water at all. It had a fence around it, which meant I did not have to worry about it when I was not around. The neighbours kept chickens and Robert, who was very little, disliked them intensely. I think he saw them as a huge threat being very large and about his height. They often wandered into our garden.

Jane had been born with a lump on the back of her head and we went to see the American Doctors at the Raleigh Fitkin Memorial hospital. I saw a very well known doctor called

Howard D Hamlyn and he was to do the operation to remove it. He gave us a date and we duly went in the night before. Poor Jane was woken up at 3.45 to have an enema (what on earth for I wondered?) then when she had just gone back to sleep she was again woken to have her head shaved in preparation. She was not allowed to eat of course so by this time I had a very unhappy little girl to keep entertained until they called us to theatre. Unbeknownst to us though Dr Hamlyn had gone to Johannesburg for a few days and on his way home the Border Police would not allow him back into Swaziland on a technicality. I decided that we would go ahead anyway and the next doctor did the operation. They gave Jane ether and she was terribly sick afterwards. It seemed to all go well until the next day when she developed a massive clot on the wound, which was going to tear the stitches. They had to take her back to theatre to drain the clot and re-stitch the wound. They let me carry her and hold her until the ether was given. She was really frightened because she knew what it was going to be like. The doctor explained to us that the cyst was a Dermoid cyst which is the remnants of a Siamese twin that had been growing in her neck muscles. It took an hour and a half to remove it all. It was full of hair and teeth. A lot of people were critical of me taking her to the local hospital instead of going to see a specialist in Johannesburg. I doubt if I would have been allowed to hold my child and carry her into theatre at one of those hospitals! I was very happy with the treatment we had received there. While we were in the hospital a baby boy was born that we all nicknamed "Big Chief Roaring Bull." He never stopped roaring and seemed to be hungry all the time. Jane called him "Moaning Bill" and couldn't bear the noise he made! Dr Hamlyn had been a top surgeon in Chicago before he got the "calling". He gave up his big practice, and packing everything up moved his whole theatre out to Swaziland. It all came by sea and then, from Durban on South African Railways. He told Ian, when it took such a long time coming, that God made all creeping things including South African Railways! He had a great sense of humour.

At about this time I went down with a really bad bout of Strep throat, which gave me Scarlet fever. I was really quite ill and had no voice, terribly swollen joints especially my hands, and could not walk with ease. I had some massive injections, which cleared up the throat, and luckily the joint swelling was only transient and did not leave me with any problems. They were looking at Rheumatoid Arthritis at one point. We all seemed to be pretty unwell during our time in Manzini and I put it down to the heat as much as anything. It was while we were there that Ian started with his kidney troubles, which were to give him a hard time for a long time. Tommy got threadworm and we all had to go on worm pills. He had been looking very thin and they had to test him for all the worms. We did have three dogs and a few cats so it's no wonder really. I knew that once we moved back up to the high veld we would all be better. But in spite of all the ailments I really liked living in Manzini. I had plenty of friends and we had a busy happy social life.

Although in summer time it was really hot in Manzini, it was quite cold during the winter. Whenever South Africa had a cold front moving through, we would be affected. I remember one time in June when there was snow as low down as Waterford school, Piggs Peak and Havelock mines at Forbes reef. Very unusual! We took the children to see it and Tommy had a lovely time playing in it and making snowballs. We did have some warm coats, which my sister had given to us, cast offs from her children who were older, but still the children got pretty cold that day. There could be a warm spell in the winter sometimes. One time when it was the Queen's birthday parade, we had one of those berg wind days when it is terribly hot. I was lucky to be dressed in a cool cotton dress and hat. I noticed lots of other women were far too warmly dressed! Ian was in his "ice-cream suit" so he was fine.

One of our dogs Scramble (who had been given to us by the Wynns from Mankayane while we were in Goedgegun) was hit by a taxi and had a broken leg. The vet put his leg into plaster and he hobbled about with that for a few weeks. When it happened he hid in a hole under the hedge and Benson had to pick him up to come for treatment. We had tried to entice him out not knowing that he was in terrible pain and could not move.

Lola the rather horrible little bitch that we were also given seemed to be permanently on heat or having puppies. I never managed to get her to the vet at the right time to have her spayed. We gave her away eventually when another batch of puppies were due and the new owners were thrilled at the idea! Our cats were also prolific breeders but we never had any trouble giving the kittens away. The children loved having puppies and kittens around. I suppose now we would be regarded as irresponsible pet owners!

One of Ian's jobs was to issue licenses for businesses or liquor outlets. He was constantly offered bribes, which of course he had to decline. He was not even allowed to keep boxes of chocolates given to us by the applicants at Christmas time. They all went to the hospital. The children took a dim view of that!

Swaziland was now preparing for Independence so Ian was away a lot making sure all the celebrations were properly prepared. We had various social things to attend to. One of them was to have the retiring High Commissioner Sir Frank and Lady Lloyd to stay and to host a big party as farewell to them. The planning for that was endless as the protocol that had to be followed was very strictly adhered to. I managed it and they enjoyed their time with us. Later we had to host the new incoming British High Commissioner Peter Gautrey and his wife Pearl. We had a huge party for them. The PWD enclosed our verandah with wood so that we could overflow onto the stoep. I ordered a Rand Club ham from Johannesburg and we had cold ham, cold beef and lots of different salads. They were very appreciative and sent me an enormous bouquet of flowers the next day. I really liked them both very much and we would see a lot of them over the next year.

The Independence parade was to be held in Manzini at the huge show grounds. There was so much to think about. All the seating, all the King's wives in the correct order of importance. It must have been a nightmare for the organisers. I know that there was a last minute problem with some of the seating but I can't remember exactly what happened. I just saw lots of women arriving and a lot of shuffling about. The ceremony was long and tedious for me as I was worried about leaving the children with the nanny for such a long time. I knew that she would have liked to be at the ceremony too and had hoped that she and the children would come with us. That certainly was not to be!

11.   Independence, and Mbabane

We had known for a while that when Swaziland became independent Ian's job would come to an end because he was white. Some of Ian's colleagues had already been sent back to the U.K. or South Africa depending where they had been recruited. It therefore came as no surprise when Ian was told he had to go and pretty well within the next month. He objected to being given such short notice so instead of his being thrown out straight away he was offered a job in the Ministry of Tourism. It meant yet another house move and we would be living in Mbabane again. I must say I was relieved to leave Manzini as we had all suffered from the heat and the climate was never going to suit us. He really enjoyed the tourism work and spent lots of time with Terry Reilly helping him to get the wild life parks off the ground.

Ian had already started to job hunt knowing what was in store for him and he had been offered a position in the Rhodesian civil service. We decided that we ought to go up and have a look at it before committing to the job. So we left the children with Creina and Greville Beattie in Mbabane and went off to Rhodesia. We were shown the place where we would live and work and we spoke to local farmers in the area. One of them had three small children and he told us that it got so hot there that the children had to sleep on the concrete floor. It was the only way they could keep them cool enough. So that really made the decision for us. There was no way we could expect our children to be brought up in that heat after Manzini. In retrospect it was just as well because of the troubles that started soon after that. Ian would have been in the thick of it all.

They had given Ian 6 months before he had to be out of Swaziland after the fuss he made when they first gave him the boot, but in fact they liked him so much in the Ministry of Tourism that they asked him if he would stay on a permanent basis. He told them that he would never work for them permanently after the way they had treated him by giving him 2 weeks to leave just a few months before. He felt he would never feel secure in his job. I think they kept on delaying our departure because they liked his work but in the end we knew we would have to leave and go back to England. He really enjoyed working in the tourism industry and we had a great time in our last year in Mbabane.

Ted Reilly who had done a good job getting it all going had developed Mlilwane and it was a lovely place to visit. He had a semi tame warthog called Lady Jane. She was huge and quite intimidating for the children but very entertaining. She loved being scratched while lying on her back. They also had a dassie which lived in the house with them. Liz had managed to house train it and it squatted on the loo when it needed to go! Some rhinos had arrived in the park earlier and had settled in well. We had seen them in their boma when they first came but now they were harder to find as they were roaming freely in the reserve. We had great fun with Terry and Liz camping on the new reserve they were developing called Ehlani. We just threw a tarpaulin down under a tree and lay there to sleep. The children had to sleep in the back of the station wagon as there were leopards about. It was in the lowveld and so was warm enough at night.

The house we had been allocated was so terrible that Ian refused to move into it. We went to stay in the Swazi Inn for two weeks while they sorted out a better house for us. We eventually were allocated a house in Mbabane, which was convenient for the school. Tommy was now ready to go to "Big" school and he was enrolled at St Marks to start in the New Year. He went off happily in his smart new uniform and soon settled into school life. The head master was Mr Brockwell and if Tommy needed to threaten us if we annoyed him he would tell us he would tell Mr Brockwell! Later when we moved to Port Elizabeth I met his son Anthony and his wife Juliet Brockwell who was also a physio and worked with me. They laughed about Tommy using his dad to threaten us!

Tommy was doing really well at St Marks and had settled in so well. He looked very thin and small but could hold his own so I knew he would be fine. The school had a good reputation and he had a very good grounding there. Robert and Jane both needed to go to a nursery school and the only way I could get them into one was for me to work in the school. I was happy to do that and did two days a week, taking them both with me so they had a bit of exposure to school that way. When they interviewed me for the position they asked me if I liked children! This seemed to me to be a definite prerequisite for working in a nursery school. I loved my time there and Robert and Jane did too. I had to be very discreet as one gets told all kinds of things by the children. Things that the parents would probably prefer not to be spoken about!

One place we never lived in was Piggs Peak but we often went there to have walks in the country. There were some good bushman's paintings that we could get to after quite a long walk. They were in fair condition. Ian had to go on business too, so we would go as well sometimes. It was a beautiful part of the country. There was a very fine waterfall and Ian and John Sturgis managed to get right down to the pool at the bottom for a swim. It was far too steep for the children and me so we pottered around picking wild flowers. We used to go out with a few friends and show them wonderful walks along the contour paths.

The house we were allocated was in a terrible state when we moved in but I did not want to wait for it to be cleaned so we moved in and Ida and I got stuck in to get it clean and acceptable. That was when I learned a lot about plumbing and how to degunge a lavatory, which had clearly been blocked for ages! The house was another ordinary little Government house with no character so I set about making it into a comfortable home for us all. We acquired a Shetland pony and another small horse. The children had great fun with them. I had never owned a horse of any sort before so I needed some help. Benson seemed to know what he was doing and he would lead the children around on the pony. Robert used to mount it by climbing up its tail. He enjoyed riding and when no one was there to help him he would help himself! We had to move the ponies to the Sturgis farm, as we did not have enough grass in the field next door to us. So that meant we had to go down the hill if we wanted to ride.

Apart from working at the nursery school I also did a locum for one of the Physios for two months at the St Michaels clinic. I loved getting back into Physio and had missed it. I did not enjoy the other staff members and found some of them lacking in good ethical behaviour. I had a few private patients of my own, which was nice for me. I would have been pleased to get into a hospital situation again though. I treated them in a room at the Private hospital. There was no phone in the room so a nurse would have to run over to call me if I had a phone call.

I had seen an advertisement in the paper for a tumbler and all the equipment needed to tumble stones. I had my own collection of agates and carnelians that I had collected over many years. I bought the tumbler and soon had it working in the garage. It had to be left on all day and night. I learned how to change the grinding powder and when to start thinking about the actual polishing. Ian had his doubts about this little enterprise of mine and he was surprised when I was so successful! I had so much fun with that machine. I ended up having to think what I was going to do with all these beautiful stones. I bought some "findings" and started to make jewellery and ornaments. A shop had just opened in Mbabane selling touristy type wares. I could not keep up with the demand and soon had quite a production line going! I made enough money to be able to buy myself a new sewing machine. It was a Bernina and was a wonderful acquisition for me. I still have that machine and it sews as well now as it did then. I used to cover empty whiskey bottles (Dimple Haig) with colourful stones and varnish that. They made very pretty lamp stands. I bought the fittings for a lamp and sold them like that. Apart from them I made bracelets, ear rings and brooches.

I was lucky enough to find a huge amount of carnelians one day when we had a puncture in Mozambique. Ian was changing the tyre and I sat on the side of the road in the cutting and realized I was seeing heaps of beautiful orange stones. So I emptied the sack of oranges I had in the car and filled the sack up with stones. I made some really attractive things with these stones! We also went to a farm on the South African border near Golela and hunted for amethysts. I found some very nice geodes there! Ian was good about taking me out with him when he had to travel about for work so that I could fossic about for stones. Swaziland has plenty of lovely jasper and I picked up a lot in the rivers. That is probably where I got bilharzia. While I was careful with the children I was not careful enough with myself! The treatment for that was not fun and I spent a whole week in bed while taking the medication.

While we were living in that house Netty came up to paint Robert's portrait. She had done the other two previously. I took her into town to the shop to take some stone things in and she spotted a wonderfully decorated woman all dressed up in her traditional clothing. She negotiated with her to come for a sitting and she painted a wonderful portrait of her. The woman had misunderstood what was going to happen and had brought a small child along with her. We had to explain that only she would be in the picture. Netty gave her some money and she was happy enough with that! Judging by all her necklaces and beadwork she was a Sangoma of note. Her hair was in sort of little plaits covered in mud and she had a headdress made of beads and porcupine quills. She had lots of feathers and little things hanging from a string around her neck.

We had a lovely holiday in Mozambique that year. Ian had always promised that we would go back one day. This time we went to Inhaca Island which is just off the coast near Lourenco Marques(now Maputo). We had to take a ferry to get across to the Island. This was the most terrifying journey. The ferry had nothing on the sides to hold onto. You sat on the hatches and I held onto the children for dear life. Poor Jane was terribly seasick and I wondered if we would ever get there. When we did arrive we had to wade through the water, as there was no jetty and the ferry anchored in the bay. Our cabin was very comfortable and we spent lots of time on the beach investigating all the new and interesting things in the sea. It's a small island and not much else on it apart from the hotel we stayed in. Ian taught the children all about sea slugs and how to use them as a water pistol! I spent the whole time we were there trying to persuade Ian to let us fly back to L.M. He was having nothing of it and we simply had to return the way we had come. The master of the ferry told us one old lady had fallen off the ferry (slipped off the hatch) and had been left to flounder in the sea since it was far too dangerous to turn the boat round to pick her up. I was horrified and was very happy to be back in L.M. safe and sound even if a bit seasick.

We drove home via Stegi and they had a ball that night so we went to the ball. It was lovely to see the Forbes again. We always enjoyed time spent with them. They had one of Peter's old teachers living in the house and she was getting very frail now. Bess was an amazing person. This teacher (Miss Fowler) came to stay for a holiday and never left so they ended up looking after her to the end. Their children were very sweet with her and regarded her as part of the family.

There was an outbreak of Foot and Mouth disease so there were roadblocks between Stegi and Manzini in an effort to contain it. Peter Forbes had a dead boom slang which he had in the back of his bakkie. When the police stopped him and asked if he had any meat he said "Yes its in the back". They opened it up and of course saw the snake and ran screaming! Peter was always teasing them and giving them a hard time. He got hold of a lion's front paw and stuck it up his sleeve and pulled it out to show his horribly mutilated hand. Some people did not think that was funny!

Soon after we got back home we had a motor accident. We were on the way to take Ian down to work after lunch. A car came out if a side street just in front of us and we hit the car head on. Luckily for us our insurance broker had been driving behind us and had seen exactly what had happened so they paid out with no problem. The man driving the other car absolutely denied that he was in the wrong!

We used to go for wonderful walks in the countryside around Mbabane. I used to look for manure for the garden while we were out. One time Jane was jumping off some rocks when she cut her foot very badly by landing on a broken bottle. I dashed home again and having cleaned up the wound, I asked Tommy to just hold the wad of cotton wool against her foot while I went to get a dressing. When I came back Jane's foot was uncovered and bleeding badly and Tommy was unconscious on the floor. I had not realized he had this aversion to the sight of blood and had fainted. It had happened before when he had cut his finger on some sharp grass and he had passed out but I never put two and two together. (He still cannot bear the sight of blood!) So I scooped both children up, put them in the car and headed to the hospital for stitching. The young doctor we saw was funny. Jane gave him a lot of backchat and complained that she could not see what he was doing. He said well you should have cut your foot on top instead of underneath! He looked Tommy over and said he seemed to be fine and was none the worse for his fainting.

My brother Robert was getting married in Cape Town to Val. Jane was to be a bridesmaid and they sent me the fabric for her dress to wear. It was bright green with little white spots. She burst into tears when she saw it having thought she would be wearing something pink and pretty! I made the dress and she looked really cute in it. Just before we were due to go down to Cape Town for the wedding one of our neighbour's children Richard Tainton decided to cut her hair for her! I was furious as we had been looking after it to make sure she would look good for the wedding. So I beat him and sent him home. He came in crying at home and June asked him why. He told her he had cut Jane's hair so she beat him too. When Al came home from work that evening and heard about it he also beat him. I don't suppose he will ever forget that day. Jane had a very short hair cut for the wedding as a result.

The wedding was great fun for us all. Ian could not come so I flew down on my own with the children. Someone else picked up my suitcase from the airport and when I got to the hotel I realised that I had picked his up. They were identical and he just grabbed the first one that came off. We contacted the airport immediately and they were able to locate the man who by this time had travelled to somewhere inland quite far away. All our wedding outfits were in that case so we had to get it back before the wedding. Luckily for us we did get it back and were able to wear what we had intended. Robert greatly entertained the people at our table by telling them that his Granny could take her teeth out. One of the bridesmaids was ill with a kidney infection so she went home pretty quickly after the wedding.

While we lived in Mbabane we all seemed to suffer from some sort of illness or other. Robert ended up having to have his tonsils removed. I had to take Tommy in with me as he had had another fainting fit and I did not want to leave him. I left Jane with a friend. They did some tests on Tommy while we were at the hospital but they could not find anything wrong with him. I was beginning to think he needed to be seen by a paediatrician and would look into that next time we were to go to Johannesburg. We did go and all they said was that he had nothing seriously wrong. He had a bad start with his stressful birth and he might take a few more years to get strong. We need not have worried! He went on to become a sturdy small boy.

I really wanted the children to swim well so I used to take them down to the Swazi Inn where there was a lovely pool and we would all swim. I met some new people who were staying at the hotel. And the children always found other children to play with. It was while staying at the Swazi Inn that I found out about the pool and the management did not seem to mind me coming. I played a lot of tennis too, which was good for me. We would play at the police tennis courts or the club where I was a member.

Benson suddenly announced he was going to leave school. He had been with us all this time just changing school each time we were transferred. Now he said he wanted to work full time, save up enough money so that he could go back to school at a later date. I often wonder if he ever achieved that after we left. It was lovely to have him every day in the garden and he was diligent at growing vegetables for us. He looked after the ponies and had lots more time to help me with the flowers. I had taken cuttings from out last house so was trying to establish another lovely garden. I always tried hard to establish pretty gardens and was getting tired of moving just as they were starting to look good.

Ian was getting very fed up with the house and had decided that we should build our own house. We started looking for plots and found a few which might have been good only to find out that the area was damp or scheduled for something else. He became despondent and stopped looking. He was increasingly finding work irksome and was already thinking about alternatives.

One year after independence, Princess Alexandra came to Swaziland for a delayed celebration. Ian had been appointed Comptroller of the Royal Household and worked hard at making her visit successful. He had to find a house to rent, a car to use and make sure she had all the comforts that she was accustomed to. Mary Fitzallen Howard was her lady in waiting and he worked closely with her with all the arrangements. He really enjoyed that very much. Princess Alexandra gave him a nice pair of gold cuff links and a photograph, which I still have.

It was at about this time that things became really difficult for Ian at work. One day they would tell him how good he was and how much they liked his work and the next tell him he had 10 days to get out of the country. He refused to be bullied into going with immediate effect and insisted on his right to a three-month notice period. So that is what was decided. We had three months and then we were on our way. That was a blow and Ian had to start seriously thinking about the future. We decided that since we had been recruited in England they could pay for us to go over to the UK where we would work and settle down. We heard that Mark Patey and lots of others had also been given very short notice but it suited them to go immediately. We started the process of leaving the country, saying goodbye to our friends and staff and making bookings for the boat trip back to England. We had to spend a few months in South Africa first so stayed at the Sunnyside Guest farm for 6 weeks before going down to Cape Town to wait for the boat. While we were waiting we went to the beach one day, leaving our jackets on the beach. The tide came in and I saw Jane staggering up the beach trying her best to save the jackets! They were still wet when we boarded and we had soggy clothes in the cabin for a few days. It was on this trip that Jane demonstrated her ability to mimic accents. By the time we arrived in England she was speaking with a broad Yorkshire accent (copying the little girl she played with on the boat.)

So that was the end of our time in Swaziland, and we became "When Wes"!

Cover illustrations:
Front: Hlatikulu house
Back: At the Manzini Residency / The Butler family with grandpa Stanley Butler

Printed in Poland
by Amazon Fulfillment
Poland Sp. z o.o., Wrocław